A MALAY VILLAGE AND MALAYSIA

social values and rural development

PETER J. WILSON

HRAF PRESS • New Haven

Library of Congress Catalog Card Number: 66-27877

Selamat Zul!

INTRODUCTION

The aim of this brief report is to concentrate attention on a specific topic: the conduct of Malay villagers in their relationships with
their outside world and the values and attitudes that underlie this conduct.
The scope of a report such as this lies somewhere between a paper and a
monograph—a more extended treatment of the theme can be given than
is possible in a paper, and yet much of the background and detailed description of an ethnographic monograph can be omitted.

The description is deliberately intended to leave out some of the
technicalities of an anthropological report and to provide instead information of a topical nature, so that the whole may prove of interest to those
concerned with the political, economic, and social development of Malaysia. Although the concentration on social interrelationships is anthropological, it is presented in the belief that any form of development must
be concerned first and foremost with the understanding and development
of people. As in the majority of countries of the so-called "third world, "
the backward segment of the population of Malaysia, and of Malaya in
particular, includes the rural sector, or the "rural masses, " as one ideology terms them. National development in any shape or form is in large
part rural development, and in Malaya the Malays are the rural sector.
The Malays of the village of Jendram Hilir, who are the subject of this
study, are in many ways typical of that segment of the Malay population
of Malaya living on the west coast and depending on rubber tapping for a
livelihood.

Any phase of development, any policy to be implemented, is
affected both by the nature and culture of those who direct development
and those to be developed. The entire process, or set of processes, is
carried out only through the interrelationships of people, and these relationships are invariably asymmetrical. The developer is an outsider to

the villager, and, as will be shown below, each outsider as he enters into relationship with a villager is categorized or pigeonholed as a variant of a stereotype. No matter how demonstrably true or false the stereotype, it provides the plan of conduct for the villager, who proceeds to follow his own definition of the situation. Thus, for example, no matter what the intentions or personality of any individual Chinese may be in any situation with a Malay, the latter will always proceed in the belief that the Chinese is an infidel—dirty, cunning, and deceitful. Equally, it may be averred that the Chinese acts according to his stereotype of the Malay—lazy, naive, and incompetent.

These stereotypes, assumptions, and ideas of appropriateness about people, their behavior, and their culture (i.e. values) are in part derived from first-hand experience and in part derived from imagination informed through various ways and means, the most important of which are described below. Basically, in Malaya at least, the villager interacts with an outsider in a formal, unidimensional status. He knows a particular Chinese or Indian or bureaucrat only as a merchant, employer, manager, clerk, or official, and not as a friend, a relative, a family man, a man with a sense of humor, or a religious believer. The gaps in the humanistic view are considerable and can be filled only by hearsay, imagination, generalization, partial observation, and restricted information. The very limited nature of interaction only feeds back into the stereotype. Nor should this proclivity toward categorization be considered either surprising or unusual. It is probably universal, but we as outsiders have a tendency to think only in terms of gross categories of "natives" (or Malays), and we are often surprised to discover the "natives" differentiating themselves into more refined categories using criteria that we may often consider irrelevant or unscientific. So, for example, Europeans may consider the racial characteristics of Chinese (skin color, epicanthic fold, face form, etc.) to be the major criteria of definition; whereas to Malays, the racial (i.e. biological) differences are quite unimportant and the Chinese passion for pork (a culture trait) is far more significant.

The first chapter describes Malay villager stereotypes of the people with whom they come into contact, and the context of contact is also described. The second chapter is concerned more with villager reaction to outside events and processes which in various ways form part and parcel of Malaysian development. The third chapter deals with the economics of the village, because of all phases of contemporary life it is this which sucks the villager into active contact with the outside world and it is the economy which is the major focus of development. However, rather than dwell on statistics and techniques, I am mainly concerned in this chapter with the nature of social relations arising out of economic activities. Finally, Chapter 4 describes the basis of social relations among villagers and the structure of village social life. This is of critical importance, since it provides the social and cultural paradigm, the ideal type, by which all social relations are judged and planned.

The use of the village as a unit of study and description is more for convenience than it is a reflection of the social structure of Malay society. The Malay village is primarily a coresidential unit, and it displays little or no unity arising out of the interlocking of social relations among villagers. Malay social relations focus on the individual rather than any large aggregate of persons, although there is some aggregation in certain spheres such as the religious and the administrative. This is, however, imposed from the outside.

The primacy of the individual in Malay social structure and the intangible nature of "values" make generalization difficult, and perhaps suspect. The rendering of a datum into a statistic by no means makes it objective or valid, although there are some who would have it so. Nowhere is this more true than in respect to values or in the attempt to describe what we think other people think. Since this report describes values and thoughts, the following study makes absolutely no claim to be definitive. Presented here are interpretations made as impartially as the circumstances of my own cultural background would allow. All information was obtained as informally as possible; no tests were administered and no formal interviews were held. Both tests and interviews have the disadvantage of presenting the informant with an abstract problem in an artificial context, so that for many purposes both are unreliable as sources of information. As far as possible, therefore, information was obtained from informal, spontaneous conversations in which I participated directly or which I overheard, especially in the coffee shop. Observed interaction and relations, some degree of direct participation in village life, and, whenever possible, direct questioning all yielded information. All work was done in Malay, an easy language to speak badly and get by on but one with many subtleties to deflate the overconfident outsider.

While the individual is the center of social relations, Malays share a common basic culture (adat) and a common religion (Islam). In the broadest sense they are a united cultural group vis-à-vis the other cultural groups of Malaysia and Southeast Asia. Consequently, except in those contexts where differences between villagers are important, it seems reasonable to assert that there is a consensus of basic values or

cultural norms. Any validity of generalization for points made below rests
on these assertions.

P. J. W.

Sunapee, N.H., 1966

ACKNOWLEDGMENTS

I would like to thank the Human Relations Area Files for not only making possible what turned out to be a most pleasant and rewarding experience but also for the pleasures of an association that has lasted several years, and which I hope will continue. Particularly with respect to their help in many and various ways in this project my sincerest thanks to C. S. Ford, Frank W. Moore, Frank M. LeBar, George R. Bedell, Elizabeth P. Swift, and Gladys G. Page. The field research on which this book is based was conducted during 1964-65 under the sponsorship of the Human Relations Area Files, allocating funds provided by the Department of Defense as part of a project for collecting and organizing ethnographic data on a number of societies.

In Malaya my gratitude to the people of Jendram Hilir is beyond the means of my expression. Especially I would like to record the thanks of myself and my wife to Datok, Moyang (Nenek), Emak (Mak), Adik, Noriah sama semua keluarga! To Penghulu Mohsin bin Mahsein go our thanks for help in his official capacity and for the delights of his friendship. Dean Robert Ho of the University of Malaya amicably extended the necessary support of that institution, thereby smoothing the way through formalities.

To Dr. Peter Chapman and family the Wilson family owes innumerable thanks for the maintenance of both our physical and social health. Peter and Inge Goethals cheered us, guided us, and stood us on our feet at a time when we were utterly inverted.

Professor Raymond Firth of the London School of Economics and John Bottoms of the London School of Oriental and African Studies gave generously of their time and knowledge, thus making preparations for the trip that much easier.

And then, to my wife, whose labors under trying field work conditions were indeed prodigious, terima kaseh banyak. She looked after me and gave birth to our first son.

ix

CHAPTER 1

Ethnic and cultural diversity and complexity is an outstanding feature of the organization of the population of Southeast Asia—a diversity admirably documented in the recently published Ethnic Groups of Mainland Southeast Asia (LeBar et al. 1964). This group diversity is further complicated by the patchwork of politically defined national boundaries being drawn, erased, and redrawn throughout the region. While simplification of this diversity inevitably leads to distortion, a reasonable generalization, adopted by most scholars who treat the region as a whole (a recent example is Burling 1965), is that which distinguishes a tribally organized population inhabiting the upland regions and a politically dominant but socially amorphous peasant population living in the lowland areas. Not only is the lowland population politically dominant but its culture dominates the politically defined nation (as in Burma, Thailand, and Vietnam) and is economically more sophisticated. Whereas the lowland population of each nation draws its cultural boundaries to coincide approximately with its political boundaries, the upland hill tribes straddle all national boundaries. Among the major problems in the development of Southeast Asian nations are reconciling the highland and lowland populations and hastening a political jell of the highland tribes.

Having crudely indicated one of the most distinctive features of Southeast Asia, I must now focus on the exception to the generalization—Malaya. Here the ethnic diversity of a politically boundaried population cannot be reduced to upland tribes versus lowland peasants. Such tribal peoples as there are in Malaya—the Jakun, Senoi, and Semang—are so few in number as to constitute only a minor welfare problem for the nation. Malaya's (and Malaysia's) national population problem resides in the possibilities for coexistence and integration of two demographically balanced but culturally distinct ethnic groups, the Malays and the Chinese. An added ingredient, though of the significance of spice rather than flour or water, is the Indian segment of the population. A viable nation can rise only from a smooth blending of these three ethnic groups, among whom there is approximate parity of sophistication, in the mastery of those elusive skills and alien ideas whose acquisition and application we term "development."

The coexistence of two or more demographically significant but culturally diverse populations within a single political unit is commonly termed a plural society. However, it may be preferable to reserve this term for a colonial situation where those sections that comprise the mass of the population have severely limited access to political power, which is vested in a fraction of the population whose power derives from outside the entire community. With the demise of the colonial power, political power in the new nation becomes available to the resident population segments, and their attempts at distribution of this power and the concomitant control of the economy, the two foundations of an independent nation, provide the mainspring and impetus for either the integration or the estrangement of the ethnic components of the national population. The study of this process is usually undertaken at a survey level, through the detailed examination of the behavior of those who possess power or who compete for power in the economic and political realms (see, for example, two recent and excellent publications—Fisk 1963; Brackman 1966). Since it is the decisions made by those who concern themselves with the exercise of power at a national level that have most influence on the course of events which decide the national and international fate of populations, it is only proper that such studies continue to occupy scholars. But ethnic diversity and politico-cultural integration concern and affect those who are subject to the decisions of politicians—the individuals who make up the anonymous segments by which we describe the national population of Malaya: the masses, to use a term from another ideology. Probably in the last analysis it is the attitudes and values of the least sophisticated toward each other that determine the success or failure of whatever policy is used to bring about the viability—cultural, economic, and political—of the new nation of Malaysia. Such attitudes and values, and the circumstances which engender them, are often the least well known and least studied, even by those directly concerned in molding them.

It is with this in mind that the remainder of this chapter attempts first to outline the historical circumstances of the materialization of an ethnically diverse population in Malaya and then to describe the reactions of Malay villagers to Chinese, Indian, and other ethnic groups who inhabit the country. The very particular historical events and contexts of the introduction of the racial groups to the territory of Malaya is crucial to the understanding of their separateness and interdependence in the contemporary setting at all levels, from the nation to the village. These

-3-

historical circumstances also give clues to the settings, which in their turn may be said to have contributed to the formation of the stereotypes that the ethnic groups have of each other. And while a stereotype is suspect as a scientific definition, it is a powerful and "truthful" definition to those who have formulated it and use it. That is to say, for example, that while the Malay stereotype of the Chinese as dirty may be demonstrably false to the anthropologist, who would never report as an ethnographic fact that the Chinese are dirty, yet it remains a valid and reportable fact that Malay villagers consider Chinese to be dirty. Malay village ethnography of the Chinese, if it existed, could report that the Chinese are dirty. Malay villagers' reactions to Chinese in general and to individual Chinese are influenced by this "fact," and it is because of this that the following description of Malay village stereotypes is important to the understanding of relations between the ethnic groups.

Our knowledge of the first settlement of "Malays" in the Peninsula is probably based as much on fancy as on fact. Malays and Indonesians apparently settled the Peninsula and archipelago at some time around 1500 B.C., after migrating from southern China (cf. Winstedt 1950: 11; Fisher 1956: 278; Gullick 1958: 7). They displaced the sparse population of aborigine peoples—Negrito, Jakun, Semang, Senoi—who moved into the hills and jungles of the interior, where they have lived in small nomadic bands up to the present time. The most likely region of early Malay settlement is the northern part, in what is today known as Kelantan, Patani, Kedah, and in the extreme south in Johore. It is likely that these areas have been continuously settled or occupied by "Malays" (cf. Fisher 1956). For a period of about 2,000 years we must presume comparatively little knowledge. The entire region was variously under the attenuated

-4-

political domination of groups ruling in China, Thailand, India, and the island empires of Indonesia (though the contemporary states denoted by these names did not, of course, exist). Probably far more reaching in its cultural influence than this geo-political contact was the extensive trade network that developed over the entire region, which caught up Arabs as well as Indians and Chinese.

> By 1400 A.D. it appears that most of modern Malaya
> and Singapore was divided into a number of small
> tribal states. Those in the northwest and along the
> east coast were under the suzerainty of Thailand,
> which itself was a titulary vassal of China, while
> those fronting on the Strait of Malacca were probably
> under the hegemony of one or other of the Sumatran
> states, who were in turn vassals of Majapahit [Ginsburg
> and Roberts 1958: 23].

The early 1400s saw the first foothold of Islam on the Peninsula. As a result of the internal struggles of the Majapahit Empire and the subsequent conquest of Tumasek (the present-day Singapore) by the Thai, the former ruler of Palembang, a Hindu named Parameswara, eventually came to settle in Malacca. With the aid of some of his subjects from Palembang, Parameswara quickly built up Malacca to a port of considerable significance. In 1405 he was recognized as the ruler of the now important Malacca by the Ming Emperor of China and was guaranteed protection against the Thai. The blossoming of Malacca under Parameswara was based on trade, as Malacca took over much of the important Javanese trade from Pasai from whence emigrated the wealthy and talented "Moorish" merchants, together with their mollahs and priests. Parameswara was converted to Islam at the age of seventy-two, and encouraged his subjects to do the same. Although this was not the first evidence of Islam in

Malaya, it was apparently the first major foothold, and from Malacca Islam slowly rippled through the rest of the Peninsula (Winstedt 1950: 34; Hall 1955: 180). It is likely that the "Moors" were Gujeratis and that Islam came to Malacca from Gujerat.

After dominating the region for a number of years during the fifteenth century, Malacca was conquered by the Portuguese in 1511, and from about this time onward Peninsula Malays fade in political significance as various European powers (Portuguese, Dutch, and British) vied with each other for political and commercial power and privilege. Javanese merchants, and especially Bugis warrior merchants from Celebes, were often successful in their contests with the Dutch, and the Bugis more or less controlled the western coast of Malaya until the coming of the British.

> One hundred and seventy five years ago, the Malay
> Peninsula was sparsely populated, politically dis-
> united and economically undeveloped. It was cov-
> ered almost entirely by dense tropical jungle and
> the inhabitants, no more than a quarter of a million,
> were Malays who lived in small settlements along
> the coasts and rivers [Jackson 1961: 1].

The states were vaguely defined according to the lines of the natural watersheds, which made up an indeterminate and uninhabited frontier zone. The economy of these states rested on the collection of dues and taxes on riverine traffic, transporting tin primarily, and on trading and piracy. Although they had a specific and well-defined structure, with an aristocracy headed by the Sultan and a hierarchy of ministers, the Malay states were of little significance as political units. The former aristocracy of Malacca was established in Johore; Pahang was a "sort of detached province under an independent ruler of non-royal descent,"

and the Sultans of Perak "persisted as a weak but independent dynasty."
During the eighteenth century, Bugis gained control of Johore, and a
branch of this dynasty was established in what became Selangor and eventually attained recognition as an independent royal dynasty. Negri
Sembilan became "a loose aggregate of independent minor states dominated by immigrant Minangkabau from Sumatra" which were united in
wars against the Bugis from Selangor and Johore during the eighteenth
century. The remaining states of Kedah, Perlis, Kelantan, and Trengganu
were under the suzerainty of Thailand (Gullick 1958: 9-10).

The coming of the British and the subsequent development of tin
mining on a large scale, together with the beginnings of plantation development, resulted in great changes for all Malays throughout the Peninsula.
The presence of economically valuable resources below the soil and the
opening up of uninhabited land meant, among other things, that the
boundaries between states had to be precisely determined to avoid quarrels
over rights of revenue collection. Friction between Malays and between
Malays and Chinese on these matters brought about the establishment of
British protection of the States. This amounted to the appointment of a
Resident, who advised the Malay ruler on all matters except those pertaining to Moslem practice and Malay customary law (adat). With the
responsibility of law enforcement, foreign negotiations, dealings with the
Chinese, and economic and political policy decisions all left to the British,
Malayan life and culture was left free to continue more or less in a self-
made direction. Since the role of the Malays in the developing modern
economy was principally as revenue and tax receivers and as cultivators,
they had little stimulus to mine ore or to enter into the trading network.
In any case, these roles were fast becoming the monopoly of Chinese and

Indian labor imported for the purpose. Although Malays grew some padi and other crops, they were accustomed to growing only enough to meet their own needs, so that any surplus was incidental rather than intentional. The establishment of estates and plantations growing coffee, sugar cane, tapioca, peppers, spices, and other crops, as well as the development of gardening to supply the needs of the immigrant labor force, were from the very beginning undertaken by the non-Malays of the Peninsula.

In 1839, Newbold published his estimates of the population of the various sultanates of the Peninsula. The Malay population was estimated at 300,000 out of a total of approximately 450,000 (quoted in Fisher 1956: 289, 313). Almost a hundred years later, the Malay population had risen to nearly two million. According to Vlieland, the Superintendent of the Census for 1931, much of the increase was the result of immigration, principally from Java and from the various regions of Sumatra. With the vast expansion of the rubber estates in the early 1900s, Javanese laborers were encouraged to come to the Peninsula. It was, however, the over-all increasing prosperity of the Peninsula, based on rubber and tin, coupled with increasing political stability and the somewhat harsh rule of the Dutch in Indonesia, that provided the main impetus for Indonesian immigration to Malaya. Probably the largest group of Indonesian immigrants was the Minangkabau from Sumatra, who settled in Negri Sembilan, Selangor, Perak, and Pahang. Other major groups listed by Gullick (1958: 25) are Bugis, Korinchi, Rawa, Mandiling, Achehnese, and Batak. Since these immigrants were Moslem and were from a similar cultural background, they could assimilate to the resident Malay population quite easily, often through intermarriage. This did not occur between Malays and the Chinese or Indian immigrants. However, as Gullick points out,

-8-

there were noticeable differences between the various groups of Malays and they were by no means always friendly to one another. The majority of these Indonesian immigrants were concentrated in the southern and western parts of the Peninsula in the states of Johore, Negri Sembilan, Selangor, and Perak. Kelantan, Trengganu, Kedah, and Perlis, which were not ceded to Britain by the Thai until 1909, received very few Indonesian immigrants, although it is likely that they received a number of settlers from the north. The fact that a majority of the ancestors of the present Malay population of Malaya probably entered the country at the same time as the Chinese and Indians is of considerable cultural and political importance in understanding various aspects of the contemporary situation.*

British protection functioned originally to ensure peace between the states and to prevent aggression by Thailand. Gradually, as belligerency decreased, the British assumed a benevolent paternalism toward the Malays. Policies were administered which were aimed at protecting the Malays against the superior economic prowess of the Chinese. Malay reservations were created which were aimed at keeping non-Malays off the land and encouraging the maintenance of the traditional Malay life. The only major induction of Malays into the changing complexion of the

---

*The recent entry of Malays into Malaya is played down in official publications and utterances. The Malaysia Year Book, 1963, for example, reports: "The Malaysians [i. e. Malays] are indigenous to the country, and as would be expected net immigration has played only a very small part in the growth of the community" (p. 45). Yet the Monthly Statistical Bulletin for December 1960 gives the following immigration figures: Malays, 4,000; Chinese, 1,000; Indians and Pakistani, 8,600; and "other races" 2,600. The supposedly indigenous status of Malays has been questioned for political purposes by Chinese politicians.

country was when Malays were taken on in the lower bureaucratic positions of the administration. But the major changes were economic, as a capitalist economy was developed, based on the export to a world market of raw materials and the import of consumer goods. Attendant on the purely economic factors were the multitude of accessory and subsidiary skills and activities, all of which were taken on by the Chinese and, to a lesser extent, by Indians, Eurasians, and British. But they were not taken on by the Malays, whom the British, with the cooperation of the Malays themselves, kept as an exclusive rural segment. The effect of this policy was "the fossilization of the rural people, most of whom were Malays" (Aziz 1964: 81).

The first regular contact between any part of Malaya (namely Malacca) and China seems to have been established by the early fifteenth century—at least there is very little reliable information about contact before that date (Purcell 1948: 17). The major influx of Chinese to the Malay Peninsula began toward the end of the eighteenth century, when Francis Light encouraged Chinese to come to the offshore island of Penang, which he had taken over from the Sultan of Kedah on behalf of the British East India Company. The island was used as a port of call for Company vessels engaged in the China trade, and Light himself introduced pepper cultivation from Sumatra, which he encouraged the Chinese to develop. The Chinese who came also took up small-scale trading. Since a comparatively large number of Chinese had been settled as farmers and traders in Java and Brunei since 1720, the settlement of Chinese in Penang could be regarded as a natural part of the regular traffic of Chinese immigrants through the region known to them as Nan Yang, or "Southern Ocean" (Jackson 1961: 8). The founding of Singapore by

Stamford Raffles in 1819 provided another opportunity for development of British advantage, which in turn required the labor and services that Chinese were ready and willing to provide. By 1840, the number of Chinese in Singapore (17,704) was greater than the number of Malays (9,318) and Indians (3,375) combined.

It was the development of the tin resources of mainland Malaya that led directly to the major influx of Chinese. Until the beginning of the nineteenth century, the comparatively small amount of tin ore produced was mined by Malays and sold by them to the Dutch (Jackson 1961: 30-31). Chinese tin mining began in approximately 1824, and, as more areas were opened up, immigration increased in momentum, particularly in the states of Selangor, Perak, and in Sungei Ujong. The Chinese communities, which were developing rapidly, were self-governing, tightly knit, and often antagonistic to one another. In fact, it was partly because of this internecine aggressiveness of the Chinese, together with the conflicts among Malays and between Malays and Chinese—all resulting directly or indirectly from conflicts of interest in tin—that the British were called in to protect the states from each other.

British military protection and political advice to the central Malay states brought relative calm and stability, which in turn permitted the opening up of new areas for tin mining. As the mining areas increased, the demand for Chinese labor also increased, and particularly in the 1880s the Chinese population grew considerably. Although most of the Chinese who came to Malaya were from the southern provinces of China, they were of different dialect groups and social aggregates, so that the term "Chinese" tends to hide the considerable cultural and social heterogeneity of the Chinese population of Malaya. It is important to note that from the beginning Chinese immigrants came to perform specific tasks, all of them of an economic nature (tin mining, plantation development, purveying and trading for the laboring section of the population), and that the common factor in the economic contexts in which they worked was that what they produced or handled was tied in to international trade. From the beginning of the modern economic development of Malaya, the Chinese have played the most instrumental role, and they still dominate Malayan economy (although a large percentage of the contemporary Chinese population contributes to the economy in only a menial sense, as coolies, hawkers, petty traders, servants, trishaw pushers, and subsistence gardeners). As has been pointed out by Tjoa Soei Hock (1963: 34-36), poverty is a word that applies to many Chinese as well as to Malays. The same author also notes that Chinese immigrants were from the beginning of their settlement in Malaya motivated toward economic success, for it was the poverty of their lives in China that pushed them to emigrate (albeit temporarily) in the first place. Freedman's observation (1959: 64) that on their arrival in Malaya Chinese were particularly adept and versed in the handling of money and therefore well suited to modern trading, a qualification lacked by other peoples of Southeast Asia, also helps us to understand how the Chinese achieved their economically pre-eminent position.

The concentration of the Chinese on mining, plantations, and trade was also instrumental in the establishment of a definite settlement pattern which placed Chinese together in what began as villages, but which, with the increase in trade, became "a rash of upstart towns scattered through the western belt" (Fisher 1956: 303). At the same time, any social contact of the Chinese with Malays was of minimal functional

-12-

necessity, since the latter lived in villages lining the rivers and gained their income from tin mining only through revenues from production and transportation. Today the settlement pattern of Malaya shows essentially an urban population of which 64 per cent is Chinese and a rural population predominantly Malay (Sendut 1962).

Even though Chinese immigration and settlement took place in Malay-ruled states, the arbitrariness of the settlements, the cultural differences, and the economic specialization, all stemming directly from British rather than Malay initiative, resulted in a political insulation of Chinese from Malays. In what might be termed the domestic realm of politics the Chinese governed themselves through regional and clan associations, secret societies, and the talents and strength of outstanding individuals such as Yap Ah Loy, the "founder" of Kuala Lumpur (Gullick 1955). Otherwise political responsibility was exercised over, and on behalf of, the Chinese by the British.

The third major ethnic group in Malaya is the Indian. Relations between India and Southeast Asia probably go back far into the prehistoric period (Hall 1955: 12), and are mainly based on trade. Chinese written sources indicate Indianized states in Malaya dating from approximately the second century A.D. In these early times, it is likely that Indian culture, particularly Sanskrit literature, was widely disseminated, and there is considerable evidence of the role and influence of Buddhism in these early contacts (Hall 1955: 19). Indian and Buddhist influence underlay the rise of the first of the well-known Sumatran/Javanese empires—Sri Vijaya, whose influence extended to Malacca and beyond. By the eleventh century, Sri Vijaya had been conquered by the Cholla kingdom of the Coromandel coast of southern India, but since at that distance effective control could not be exercised, the constituent colonies of Sri Vijaya hived off to achieve some degree of independence. This was especially the case with the Sumatran state of Jambi, which gained control over Kedah, Langasuka (roughly the modern Perak), Trengganu, Kelantan, and Pahang (Ginsburg and Roberts 1958: 21). Generally speaking, though, there seems to have been a period of simmer before the Javanese kingdom of Majapahit arose to dominate the area in the fourteenth century. It is from this early period of Indian influence that many Malay words of Sanskrit origin, court ceremonials, and literary symbols entered into Malay culture.

Ties with India after this date were of little importance or influence, although trading still continued. It was not until the coming of the British to Malaya that the seeds of modern Indian influence were sown. The island of Penang was taken over as a settlement of the British East India Company and was governed direct from Bengal. Prior to 1800, the island was used principally as a penal settlement, and immigrants and traders, mainly from South India, were able to come and go quite freely, as there was regular contact between the island and mainland India. Merchants, boatmen, coolies, and others came to settle in Penang, and although a large number stayed there and in Kedah many also returned to India after staying for varying lengths of time (Jackson 1961: 8). This early Indian settlement was quite spontaneous and was part of the normal traffic between districts of British India until 1867, when the Straits Settlements of Singapore, Penang, and Malacca became a Crown Colony, independent of Indian concern.

Indian labor had been brought in to work sugar plantations, but the conditions of their transport and recruitment were far from satisfactory.

This led to gradual direct interference by the Indian government. The demand for Tamil labor on the European-owned estates was never satisfactorily fulfilled, partly because of inefficient recruiting methods, partly because of competition from Ceylon and Burma, and partly because only a small proportion of Tamil coolies stayed in Malaya for any length of time (Jackson 1961: 97).

Until the mid 1890s, the major estate crop in Malaya was coffee, but at that time the world price for coffee plummeted. Beginning in 1896, rubber was planted extensively, and the cultivation of that product quickly became the major concern of estates. The world demand for rubber rose rapidly during the first decade of the present century, mainly because of the development of the automobile industry, and as a result of this increasing development of rubber estates the demand for estate labor grew. Following the precedent of the previous century, estate labor was recruited from the Tamil population of southern India, and it was during this period that the greatest number of Indians entered Malaya. Not only were they brought in to work on estates but, since immigration was under government supervision, they were also brought in as labor employed by the government for roads and other construction work.

Thus, like the Chinese, the Indians came to Malaya to perform specific roles in the developing economy, thereby gaining a foothold and soon a monopoly of those roles, which have increased in national importance as a modern state and economy have formed. The contemporary Indian population is almost exclusively occupied in estate labor, government service (especially the Public Works Department), and with supplying the specialized needs of their own community (religious personnel, retailers, etc.). Their relatively independent economic and social roles

-15-

did not require that they live interdependently with either the Malays or the Chinese, so that, like those groups, they have pursued their own social and cultural lives. Although the majority of Indians in Malaya are Tamil, there are also significant numbers of Moslem Pakistanis and a small but prominent number of Sikhs. Even though the broad lines of Indian settlement in Malaya admit of some generalization, such influences as the unequal distribution of wealth, the different regions of origin, and different levels of education have led at least one writer to comment that: "there have [sic] been no unity amongst the Indians in Malaya" (Netto 1961: 55).

The thread common to the modern history of the three major groups in Malaya is that the British were responsible for the patterns that emerged. It was only through the British that the three groups, as a politically viable population, were united. The details of the economic and political roles of the three groups result from the self-generated impetus of the economic development of mining and trade, rubber and estates, and subsistence farming. Contact between the masses of the three groups has from the beginning been only formal, and the extent of their interdependence has been minimal. Thus not only are the masses of the three major groups domiciled apart—Chinese in towns, Malays in villages, and Indians on estates—but they are also culturally apart, each having been able to perpetuate the culture of the homeland, since no one of the three cultures was significant from a political viewpoint. This role was taken by British culture, and the only effective contact between representatives of the three ethnic groups has been at a rare level (principally within the professions) where Indians, Malays, and Chinese have all learned and adopted British culture, or postures of it. Until recently the lingua franca

-16-

has been English, but this has not been the language of the masses and is not a language of any of the ethnic groups. Modern information media such as cinema, radio, and literature have only recently been readily accessible to the mass of population. Those most deeply buried within their native culture—and these are the majority—have, therefore, had little or no first-hand acquaintance with each other, and their ideas of each other are derived from dubious and faulty sources of information. These ideas are of a general nature, based on a few details more or less filtered through at random and coagulated as stereotypes. Such stereotypes have the sanction of being time-honored, since until very recently the chance for their contradiction has not come about, nor has there been any perception of the need for their contradiction. With the modernization of Malaya and with Independence, the chance for contact between the masses of members of the three ethnic groups has enlarged, but the relationships, as they are undertaken by individual members, are guided by the stereotypes which were formulated in colonial times and which were learned as part of the normal course of socialization in the communities of the respective groups.

The remainder of this chapter is an attempt to draw the stereotypes that village Malays have of Chinese and Indians and of other Malays as they are manifest in the village of Jendram Hilir and to delineate the sources and the type of information from which the stereotypes have been derived.

I shall first describe some of the ideas that Malays have of each other. These are based primarily on the acquaintance of people of the village with the inhabitants of neighboring villages, so that an indication of the Malay composition of the villages surrounding Jendram Hilir will

convey not only the heterogeneity of the Malay composition of the area
but also an idea of the sources of information on which opinions are
founded.

The village of Jendram Hilir has been settled for about sixty years,
and neighboring villages within a five-mile radius have been settled for
about the same length of time, with the exception of the nearest village,
Jendram Ulu, which was founded about a hundred years ago. The region
settled by the Malays has been set aside as Malay reservation, but it is
surrounded on all sides by Chinese- and European-owned rubber plantations. A small area reserved to Senoi aborigines borders the northwestern
tip of the Malay reservation.

Jendram Hilir itself includes among its inhabitants members of three
distinct Malay groups: Mandiling, Ramba, and Kepunohan. These groups
originated in Sumatra, but I might note that I was unable to establish the
place of origin of the latter two groups and have not come across mention
of them elsewhere. In terms of village composition, the three groups
established a separate identity by tracing a common descent from specific
ancestors, but although they tend to be concentrated in specific parts of
the village, these groupings are important only in certain of the informal
political affairs of the village (Wilson 1966). Ramba and Kepunohan, as
groupings, form an alliance, since they are descended from two pairs of
brothers and sisters. They are opposed to the Mandiling, who, in turn,
claim the use of the title "Raja" to indicate a certain social superiority
to others of the village. Other Mandiling Malays live in the village of
Sungei Marab, which can be reached by a two-mile walk through a rubber
estate and secondary jungle. The village of Sungei Marab is considerably
more prosperous than Jendram Hilir, and the majority of the well-off

-18-

villagers are Mandiling. A number of the Mandiling of Jendram Hilir
are also better off than many other inhabitants, and it is they who take,
and often hold, the initiative in political affairs relative to the administration (the acting headman, for example, is Mandiling). Although this
possible superiority is not openly bragged about, the general observation
is often made in the appropriate context that, compared to some other
Malays, Mandiling are socially superior and a better class of persons. On
the other hand, the two other groups of Jendram Hilir villagers are openly
snide toward the Mandiling, and a number of individuals consider them
to be pushy and coarse. Particular sarcasm is directed against the tendency of the Mandiling people in the village to cooperate closely with the
administration in the persons of the penghulu and the district officer.

A certain superiority over other Malays is also claimed by Minangkabau living in the area. The neighboring village of Jendram Ulu is
populated almost exclusively by Minangkabau, who settled there directly
from Sumatra. This village also is manifestly more prosperous than some
of its neighbors. The government built some canals and sluices as part
of a large-scale irrigation plan, which was eventually dropped. As a
result, some 280 acres of padi fields (sawah) are well irrigated and cultivated by the inhabitants. They also own rubber smallholdings and fruit
orchards (dusun), which produce a surplus of fruit that is sold in the market at Kajang, the district capital. The main part of the village, where
the houses follow the line of the road, includes half a dozen stores, a
mosque, a school, and clinic, and a number of hamlets and homesteads
set among the padi fields off the road. Although they do not practice the
adat perpateh that is followed by the Minangkabau of Negri Sembilan, the
Minangkabau of Jendram Ulu speak the Minangkabau dialect, which is

not well understood by other Malays (such as those of Jendram Hilir), and this inhibits contact between the villages. Proportionately, there are many more families in Jendram Ulu whose members have achieved secondary educations and work at administrative and bureaucratic jobs, which carry much prestige among all Malays. This general level of achievement, coupled with an economic superiority that is in many cases quite clearly marked, causes other Malays to envy the Minangkabau in general and the people of Jendram Ulu in particular. This envy is based also on the fact that most of the Malays who are settled alongside the main Kuala Lumpur-Seremban road and many of those who are engaged in commerce in Kuala Lumpur and in the bureaucracy are Minangkabau. Another feature of the Minangkabau, imputed to them by the Malays of Jendram Hilir, is their exclusiveness. It is claimed that the Minangkabau are too snobbish to marry other Malays, and that they are, therefore, for the most part endogamous. I have no statistics to test this claim, but a preference for endogamous marriage was expressed by all the Minangkabau informants with whom I spoke.

Although they are about a fifteen-minute walk apart, or a three-minute bus ride, contact between the two villages of Jendram Hilir and Jendram Ulu is minimal. People of Jendram Hilir will not attend the weekly government clinic conducted in Jendram Ulu. Some of the reasons given are: "We cannot understand what they say" (i.e. the people of Jendram Ulu), "They [the Jendram Ulu villagers] laugh at us when we go there because we do not have fine clothes," "I do not feel comfortable [hati tidak senang] when I go there," "I do not have the time," "The medicine is no good, Chinese medicine is better"; or "The nurse talks brusquely [kasar]." (An identical reaction to government nurses is reported

by Wolff 1963.) There is a rubber-buying shop in Jendram Ulu that pays
the same price as that given by the Chinese in Kajang, Bangi, and Dengkil,
which price is higher than that paid in Jendram Hilir. It is managed by
a Malay, but owned by a Chinese. Nevertheless no one from Jendram
Hilir has ever been known to sell their rubber in Jendram Ulu, even though
the Malay who manages the shop actually resides in Jendram Hilir. A
variety of reasons are given: that it is more convenient to go to Bangi or
Dengkil because one can buy the things one needs there, as well as selling
the rubber (which one cannot do at Jendram Ulu); that although he is
Malay, the manager of the store in Jendram Ulu has faulty scales, so it is
not a good place to sell; or that "people stare at me when I go to Jendram
Ulu." For their part, many of the inhabitants of Jendram Ulu hold the
people of Jendram Hilir as a whole in disdain, mentioning their inability
to get on well with each other (referring to the factioning within the village) and describing them, as a whole, as bumpkins (bodoh). A final,
widely-held claim to Minangkabau superiority is based on physical appearance. Many of the Minangkabau of Jendram Ulu and others of my acquaintance have pointed out that they are of a light complexion and have
more refined (halus) features than other Malays, particularly Javanese
Malays.

   The village of Sungei Buah, situated a mile off the road, is populated entirely by Malays of Javanese origin. The village has a nucleus
centered around the mosque and a number of houses scattered among the
padi fields laid out within the narrow, closed valley that more or less cuts
off the village from the outside. The houses of the village are quite no-
ticeably different from those found in Jendram Hilir, Jendram Ulu, and
Sungei Marab, having a semi-closed verandah in front rather than a front

-21-

room and a rectangular, one-level floor plan instead of the "L" or "T" floor plan, with a ground-floor kitchen, that is found in the other villages. The houses of Sungei Buah are uniformly unpainted, and most are in a poor state of repair, comparing unfavorably with the well-kept houses of other Malay villages. The Javanese produce a surplus of padi and also derive considerable income from rubber. The villagers own corporately a fish tank, which is used primarily to supply their own needs, and the majority of households earn a supplementary income by burning charcoal, selling coconuts, collecting and selling timber, making furniture, and providing coolie labor, although none of these occupations is ever performed on a full-time basis. In contrast to the village of Jendram Ulu, the villagers of Sungei Buah have dug their own irrigation canals and built their own dam, bringing water to the padi fields from the nearby Semenyih river.

The people of Jendram Hilir have virtually nothing to do with Sungei Buah. No more than nine people have ever visited the village, although it is only four miles away. At various times they have purchased charcoal and other items from the Javanese of Sungei Buah, but this is about the extent of contact. For the most part, the people of Sungei Buah sell their products in Kajang. The most frequently given reason for not going to Sungei Buah is that the Javanese are dirty, that to go to the village is in itself an unpleasant experience. A somewhat grudging admiration for the capacity of the Javanese to work hard is accorded. They are likened to the Chinese in this respect and in the less complimentary (in Malay terms) respect that the Javanese, although supposedly Moslem, are given to eating pork on occasion. It is also claimed by some of the Malays of Jendram Hilir that the Javanese have different customs (adat), so that

-22-

marriage with Javanese is frowned on. In this respect it was pointed out that one of the Banjarese living in the village was married to a Javanese girl (Banjarese being probably the most despised of Malay groups).

There are two Banjarese families living in Jendram Hilir, and they are virtually isolated from all social life in the village. Banjarese, according to the stereotype held of them by Jendram Hilir villagers, are fundamentally evil and can never be trusted: they are especially prone to stealing and lying. When I was seen talking to one of the Banjar men of the village, a number of my neighbors took it upon themselves to warn me about associating with him because he was Banjar. The two families were living in the village as squatters and, whether by coincidence or because the stereotype is indeed reasonably accurate, one of the Banjar men was imprisoned in Seremban for theft soon after my arrival.

Although the distinctions between the various Malay bangsa or groups living within the immediate vicinity of the village are quite explicit, their relevance is determined by their context. Only in local day-to-day affairs which involve Malays are the stereotypes meaningful. In any contact which involves a non-Malay, the distinctions vanish, and all Malays are equal in opposition to the non-Malay. (Possibly the only exception to this, at least for the people of Jendram Hilir, is the distinction of the Banjarese, for whom there seems to be an overriding dislike and intolerance.) Opinions about non-Malays are drawn in broad, crude lines and seem to hold regardless of context. Whereas, for example, it might be admitted that there are individual Banjarese who are to be trusted, individual Chinese and Indians are always seen to represent the totality. Even a Chinese man living in Jendram Ulu, speaking fluent Malay, and living most of his day-to-day life with Malays could not overcome the stereotype

-23-

of Chinese. The comparative success of his fruit growing was seen, not as the result of his own endeavor, but as the result of his being Chinese, having the right contacts (for marketing the fruit), and possessing some sort of ill-defined secret. Although he is accepted into the coffee-drinking groups that occupy their regular tables in the coffee shop, and even though his sense of humor is greatly appreciated by the Malays, whenever he leaves the table and is out of earshot his accent is mimicked and there is a noticeable relaxation among the men.

The attitude toward Chinese, and toward Indians too, is of a far greater intensity and depth than the attitudes of Malays to themselves. The individual is inevitably seen to conform to, and thereby confirm, the stereotype, instead of the stereotype being a flexible and general approximation, as it is for Malays viewing Malays. Except for the one man in Jendram Ulu and one old Chinese man living in Jendram Hilir, there are no Chinese living in the kampong. All the Chinese live in the small towns of Bangi and Dengkil, the two towns situated at opposite ends of the mukim, or parish. Contact between village Malays and town Chinese is frequent and uniformly of an economic nature. In fact, although the villagers do not see it in this way, they are totally dependent on the Chinese for their very survival. Chinese buy all the rubber produced in the village and Chinese sell, directly or indirectly, almost all of the food consumed in the village and almost all of the other products used in the village. Since economic relations must of necessity be formal, unsentimental, and devoid of "feeling," there is little or no opportunity for Malays and Chinese to go beyond the required anonymity to see each other as more complete persons. Thus any idea that Malay villagers have of Chinese as beings of feeling is inferred by them from their relations with

Chinese as economic status holders. These inferences are uniformly harsh and unfavorable.

Malay villagers appear to hold to the opinion that all Chinese are dirty (kotor). The principal meaning implied is not so much physical dirtiness as ritual impurity, and this attitude finds its most powerful, symbolic expression in the contrast between the Malay injunction against the eating of pork because it is unclean and the extreme penchant of the Chinese for pork. Since the Malays are not, on the whole, theologically inclined, their idea of devoutness tends to hinge upon the most positive and clearly-defined injunctions of Islam as they occur in everyday behavior. Of these, the eating of pork is one of the most immediate criteria for distinguishing the chosen from the infidel. Thus, no matter how clean a Chinese may be, he is always ritually impure to the Malay. But Chinese are also described as being dirty from observations based on the conditions of living of Chinese families in small towns such as Bangi and Dengkil. Here again the contrast between the village Malay and the Chinese with respect to the value placed on the house is a most important factor. To the Malay, the house is a place of worship (as it is to the Chinese also) and it is also the center of each Malay individual's personal world. The house, its furnishings, and its inhabitants are a source of pride and an object of ambition for the Malay, so that the house, however "poor," is always clean and tidy. This does not mean to say, however, that within the village there is competition for prestige based on the elaborateness of housing. (For a further discussion of the Malay house, see Chapter 4, p. 116-17.) For the Chinese urban dweller there does not appear to be the same concentration of worldly and ritual attitude on the house as there is for the

Malay kampong dweller (cf. Freedman 1957: 51-52), although the house is clearly important to the Chinese. Thus the general untidiness and squalor of the Chinese kitchen (usually situated at the back of the shop, and the only room open to view) leads the Malay to infer that basically the Chinese house and the Chinese people are dirty. Villagers report, for example, that Chinese do not bathe — whereas Malays bathe two or three times a day.

It is, of course, in the economic realm that the Chinese and Malays come most into contact, and it is on the basis of their interaction there that mutual opinions and attitudes are formed. With respect to this field of relationships, and contrary to generalizations sometimes made by Western observers, the Malays of Jendram Hilir readily admit the superiority of the Chinese in economic affairs and, on the whole, they do not begrudge or envy the Chinese his paramount position. That many Chinese are wealthy whereas most Malays are poor is indeed a topic of concern and self-pity for Malays, but the skill of Chinese businessmen and their ability to meet all the demands placed on them are often the subjects of admiration on the part of village Malays. In the same way, the evident ability of the Chinese to work harder than the Malays is admitted and admired. One old lady in the village employed two village carpenters to rebuild her house, and from the day the operation began she regretted it and complained about their work, bemoaning the fact that she had not employed a Chinese contractor. While his superior economic prowess is acknowledged, the Chinese is also regarded as fair game for Malay trickery, in part because it is thought that he will stop at nothing in his attempt to secure a good bargain. On their return to the village after a shopping expedition in Kajang, the families of Jendram show off their purchases to relatives and neighbors, giving a running account of the bargaining that took place and ending with the announcement of the price paid and a conclusion that they beat out the Chinese storekeeper. To receive the compliment "pandai beli" (well bought) is always flattering for the Malay. A similar attitude is noted by Swift among the Malays of Jelebu. He writes: "The Chinese is regarded as fair game: cheating and theft from the Chinese are rather a joke" (Swift 1965: 66). Since women do most of the shopping, especially for cloth and household articles, this attitude is mainly characteristic of Malay women.

The number of Chinese who actually have any direct contact with Jendram Hilir is very small. They include the suppliers of the two village stores, including one from Dengkil who makes daily delivery of fish and vegetables, and the various suppliers from Kuala Lumpur who deliver items such as cigarettes, coffee, biscuits, and canned goods. Their relations with the storekeeper are quite formal, though pleasant, but only in the case of the regular supplier is there anything like a meaningful exchange of sentiment. When deliveries to the main village store are made (mostly during the morning), members of the village geng (a peer group of young unmarried men) are seated outside talking or listening to the radio. When the Chinese suppliers arrive, the geng invariably make sarcastic comments among themselves: "Here comes flat face with the leftovers [sisa]"; or "Here comes big strong biscuit seller who leaves his fly open because he has nothing to hide." When one Chinese cigarette wholesaler came with a new brand of cigarettes, he offered them around to all who were in the store. The geng members each took a cigarette, lit it, and then they all very deliberately pulled a face of disgust, spat, and ground out the cigarette on the floor. Afterward they swore that it was not tobacco

-27-

but sayor china (i.e. Chinese vegetable, also meaning excrement in its oblique reference to the use of night soil by Chinese vegetable growers).

There is one other regular Chinese visitor to the village, a store-keeper from Kajang who comes once a month to collect the payments on radios and bicycles from the thirteen village customers still in his debt. He is an unusually large man, and he always comes accompanied by his wife—a strategy which he uses in part for his own protection to ensure a polite reception. The collection of his dues is rarely a straightforward transaction, and he is inevitably subjected to much teasing in the form of excuses for not being able to pay ("I cannot pay you this month because the radio does not work properly," "I've been paying you for so many months I must have bought another radio! —Where is it?" or, from a customer who is paying for a bicycle, "I cannot pay you because everyone is sick," "I have no money this month as my trees are fasting," "Oh, the government will pay you this month," and so on and so forth). Unless there is genuine difficulty in meeting payments, the installments are paid after the teasing is over. When the difficulty is real, the storekeeper often allows deferment or agrees to accept rubber instead of cash. As a result of his policy, which is obviously adjusted specifically to dealing with village Malays, this particular storekeeper probably sells his goods to more Malays than any other storekeeper in the area. A similar point is made by Swift in more general terms, describing Malay-Chinese relations in Jelebu: "The importance of knowledge or trust [between Malay and Chinese] cannot be overstressed. . . . There is not sufficient moral community between Malays and Chinese for them to have prolonged economic relations requiring trust without some particularistic tie" (Swift 1965: 66). Relative to this point also are the reactions of some Chinese

-28-

whom I invited to the village. They all expressed a fear of coming to a Malay village house, especially in a village where they were not known, believing they might be set upon and robbed.

The relations between Malay villagers and Chinese are highly selective, limited, and glancing. There is little or no contact of any personal nature such that each meets the other in a domestic role. The only emotional contact occurs at the adoption of Chinese girls by Malay villagers (there are four Chinese-born girls growing up as Malays in the village). But the attitude of the Chinese who reject children is so distasteful to Malays that it serves only to confirm their opinion of Chinese as being devoid of that warmth and consideration for human feeling that is so important to Malays. In addition to the lack of personal relationships between Malays and Chinese and the lack of opportunity to develop them, the manifest features of Chinese culture, especially Chinese writing, create a barrier between individuals of the two races. Malay customers cannot understand Chinese reckoning, pricing, script, or language in general. They regard this strange writing as a device to cheat them and not as a legitimate and natural means of communication of the Chinese. This fact was constantly verbalized whenever the subject of marketing came up in conversation, followed by the corollary that all Chinese should use only Malay. The public evidences of Chinese culture—especially music, funerals, and other ritual celebrations accompanied by Chinese paraphernalia, are of interest to villagers, but rather in the sense of exotic and primitive practices. And although the virtues of Chinese industry and skill are genuinely appreciated by many villagers, they see no need to emulate them, since such aptitudes are inherently Chinese and naturally alien to Malays. It follows from this that Malays of the village do not appear to resent Chinese prosperity in any general way, although they are envious of the wealth supposedly accumulated by Chinese and the latter's ability to purchase automobiles and other modern equipment.

Contact between Malay villagers and Chinese is an inevitable part of daily life in Malaya, but, as has been noted, this contact is limited in its scope. Contact between Malays and Indians is by no means as regular or inevitable. There are two Indians living in Jendram Hilir — one a storekeeper married to a Malay woman, and the other a coffee house owner. However, their position is somewhat anonymous. Neither one ever leaves his house or store and interacts with any villager outside of the formal proprietor—customer relationship. Most of the clientele of the storekeeper are from the small, satellite village in the interior or from the Senoi village. Very few villagers buy goods from him, preferring to deal with the Malay-owned store. The coffee shop is used by members of the minority faction in the village and by visitors to the village (Chinese rubber collectors, wholesalers, and officials). Relations between the proprietor and villagers are not strained, they are simply not familiar. Village ideas about Indians are derived from general observation rather than any acquaintance, and they are thought of as being inferior in the sense that Indians are simpler or more primitive than either Malays or Chinese. In conversations with villagers in which I attempted to elicit opinions and judgments about Indians, the following were the features regularly mentioned. In general, villagers seem to regard Indians as people to laugh about: the blackness of skin, hairiness, and the skinny men and fat women seemed to amuse them most. The liking of Indians for bright, flat colors is, by comparison to the Malay preference for blends, patterns, and subtlety, in poor taste and receives little admiration. On the other hand,

Malay village women buy most of their cloth from Indian storekeepers, who have a monopoly on such trade. Village men and women alike object to, or find most peculiar, the smells associated with Indians. Most Indian stores have an incense stick burning, and there is often blended in with this the smell of scent. The smell of Indian cooking seems characteristic to Malay villagers, to whom the body smell of Indians is also oppressive. A major reason given by villagers for not traveling on a bus at night is that the smell of Indians is so strong. The position of Indian women is something of a puzzle to villagers, who have seen women laborers working in road gangs. Many of these women are elderly, and their ability to do such heavy work in such heat is a source of some amazement. As with the Chinese, the Indians are thought of as being dirty by comparison to Malays. But whereas Chinese are ritually or mystically dirty, Indians are considered squalid.

For their squalidness and general "simplicity," the Indians are often compared with the Senoi (or "Sakai," as village Malays refer to them). As mentioned, there is a small Senoi reservation near Jendram Hilir, and the inhabitants come to the village to buy odds and ends, sell a little rubber and some of the jungle products (animals, rattan, honey, etc.) that they have collected. Most of what they sell, however, is to the Chinese. There is, then, some contact between Malays and Senoi, who are regarded as the most inferior of human beings. The greatest insult one can incur is to be compared to a Sakai. Although there are a number of examples of conversion of Senoi to Islam and of intermarriage, the relations between the villagers of Jendram Hilir and the Senoi are quite superficial, and the relations with Indians only slightly more meaningful, even though some of the "Indians" are Pakistani and Moslem.

During the course of their day-to-day lives within the village,
the people of Jendram Hilir do not come into contact with other racial
groups present in Malaysia: the British and the tribal groups of Sabah
and Sarawak. But certain villagers have, at various times, had some
contact with these groups, most frequently within the context of the
armed forces. Formerly, contact with British personnel was fairly frequent, but today it is almost nonexistent.

Nevertheless, the white man's world impinges onto the thought of
all villagers, although it is often purveyed to them through the Chinese.
The chief source of information about the outside world and the world of
the white man in particular is old newspapers and magazines. The newspapers that have been supplied to the store by a Chinese agent are used
to wrap food and goods. They come from places as far away as England,
Holland, Scandinavia, Los Angeles, San Francisco, and Australia. The
reading matter cannot be understood, but the advertisements and photographs are always examined with the greatest interest. Such information
is, of course, quite idealized and serves to bolster the impression gained
from observation of the lives of white people in Malaya that life in such
countries is indeed luxurious. Other items, such as illustrated calendars,
are closely looked at and often highly prized as decorations, and these
too provide the same sort of clues as newspapers. More and more, however, calendars are being provided by Malaysian firms featuring Malaysians, though still posed and set in a Western pattern. Other impressions
of white men derive from individual experience of particular administra-
tors and of army and police officers. This experience is a completely
masculine one, and many villagers conceive of the white man's world as
a world without female influence or participation. Consequently, the

white man is thought of only as a formal, impersonal robotlike figure. Thus, when the National Language Competition for non-Malays was won by an American Peace Corps girl and was widely reported in all news media, the most interesting aspect to the people of Jendram Hilir, those who were interested in the matter at all, was that the winner was a white female. This event also made a significant impression because villagers attach considerable importance to the speaking of Malay as a criterion for judging non-Malays, a topic to be discussed elsewhere. In sum, it may be said that the white man (orang puteh) is a distant, almost fictional being who represents or symbolizes a world far removed from the village yet inexplicably related to the life of the village.

Of far greater importance to villagers is their relationship to Indonesians. Again, the contact is not particular, but is essentially abstract. Since the Confrontation between Malaysia and Indonesia, however, it has become an abstract that plays a role in reality. A number of the older people of the village were actually born in Sumatra, and most of these and some of their children have visited kinfolk in Sumatra. Prior to Confrontation, many kept up a correspondence with their kinsmen. For many villagers, therefore, Indonesia is not an abstract generality, a country that exists somewhere far away. It is a concept translatable into personal kinship relations between individuals. The comparatively recent immigration into Malaya of many of the people of Jendram Hilir and of other Malays of their close acquaintance (affinal relations, for example) also means that Indonesia, and particularly Sumatra, is looked on by many as the authentic source of Malay culture, much of which has been foregone but not dismissed by the villagers. As can be judged from the above outline of the ethnic composition of the mukim, most villages are made up of

populations who are culturally more dissimilar to the people of Jendram
Hilir than are the villages of Sumatra from whence the villagers originated.
I suspect that because so many of the people of Jendram have within their
own lifetimes given up many of their cultural skills and customs (such as
playing of musical instruments, dances, ritual, etc.), their respect for
people who still carry them on is greatly increased. The people of the
states of Kelantan and Trengganu are likewise respected as a category for
their maintenance of what the people of Jendram Hilir regard as authentic Malay culture (adat betul). Thus during the time of Confrontation,
the attitude of villagers to Indonesia was far from belligerent. In spite
of constant radio propaganda, police road blocks, and armored cars
patrolling through the village, the general opinion in the coffee shop
was that Indonesians and Malays would not fight one another (they were
saudara, even keluarga, i.e. kinsmen) and the whole affair was a mon-
strous joke perpetrated by Subandrio, Aidit, and the Chinese, principally
Lee Kuan Yew, Prime Minister of Singapore. The latter, it was believed,
was seeking a way of ridding Singapore of its Malay population. News
broadcasts and programs from Radio Djakarta were listened to as regularly
as those from Radio Malaysia, and an interesting sidelight on the appeal
of individuals with respect to their cultural personality is shown by the
reactions of villagers to President Sukarno of Indonesia and Prime Minister
Tunku Abdul Rahman of Malaysia. As Prime Minister, the latter received
patriotic respect (his picture was on show in a number of houses in the village), but as a Malay he was frequently derided and spoken of as being
more like an orang puteh than a Malay, especially with regards to the
somewhat slow and halting way he spoke over the radio. Sukarno, on the
other hand, whose delivery was emotional and colloquial, was viewed

-34-

as being a far more authentic Malay person.

Knowledge of other outsiders is variable. A few men of the village who are in the Army Reserve have been to Sabah and have met representatives of the indigenous tribal peoples. Insofar as they expressed any opinion about these people to me, or among themselves, it was vague—the comparison is usually made with the Senoi. On the other hand, all of the younger men carried in their wallets pictures of bare-breasted Dayak girls, whom they greatly admired as a kind of pin-up. Sabah and Sarawak, it seems reasonable to say, are blank spots to the people of Jendram Hilir.

A number of people of the village, both men and women, have made the pilgrimage to Mecca (haj). Arab culture and physical appearance provide an ideal, though abstract, standard of beauty. Although there is no desire to change Malay culture, it was pointed out to me that Arabic poetry is the most beautiful and the Arabic language also the most beautiful. Arabic music is the most appreciated by the older people of the village, although the younger ones prefer the semi-Westernized romantic ballads—principally because of the words which they could learn and then sing. Finally, the lighter skin, straight nose, and thin lips of the Arab are regarded as criteria by which beauty should be measured.

Anyone who is an outsider interacting with a member of the village is a representative of one of the stereotypes outlined above, and is prejudged as such irrespective of the individual qualities he may possess. The boundary of the unit of the stereotype is racial rather than residential, and the term used by villagers is bangsa. A bangsa varies according to context, so that within Jendram Hilir there are three bangsa, and to all people of Jendram Hilir there are various other outside bangsa: Minangkabau,

-35-

Jendram Ulu, bangsa orangorang Java, bangsa China, and so forth. It is, of course, possible for individuals to break out of the cast of the stereotype to which they belong, but this can only be done through the establishment of personal relations and only on the terms by which Malay interpersonal relations are conducted. Interpersonal conduct may be dichotomized, as may be so much else of Malay culture, into that which is halus or refined, and that which is kasar or coarse. All non-Malay bangsa are by definition kasar, and the slightest deviation or inappropriateness in behavior on the part of a non-Malay will be taken as confirmation of the kasar definition of the race. Malays, too, may be described as kasar, but with the reservation that those same Malays who may behave kasar also have it within their power to be halus. That non-Malays can be halus is always in doubt.

It is typical of the villagers of Jendram Hilir that they classify themselves and outsiders in numerous ways according to social context. These classifications—or perhaps they are better described as categorizations—if considered simultaneously, cross-cut each other and indeed may contradict each other in some instances, as when a village Malay may be described as being kasar when compared to other villagers, but halus when compared to a Chinese. Such a tendency to multiple classification according to variable and often quite seemingly trivial and irrational criteria is probably a widespread feature of "peasant" populations—at least there seems little reason to consider Jendram Hilir atypical in this respect. Depending on the commentator's moral stance, this phenomenon is often described as "prejudice"—in which case villagers of Jendram Hilir may be described as having a number of prejudices for and against people with whom they come into contact. Classification of outsiders seems to be a

-36-

response to the situation that arises out of the nature of contact between villagers and outsiders where the latter exercise most of the initiative and control and derive this prerogative from sanctions alien to the village. From the villager's point of view his categorization clarifies the relationship and redefines it in village terms and at the same time places the villager in the advantageous position in the status relationship. If outsiders are kasar, then villagers are halus, hence they are superior. It also follows from this that in their interaction, villager and outsider define the situation and their position in it somewhat differently. In other words, villagers may seem to "put on a front," but we must be careful to note that when they do put on a front, they are not so detached from it as to view it in this way. The "front" is an integral part of the whole.

The distinctions based on race or bangsa comprise one general form of classification of people employed by villagers. Still another is based, in general, on the status of people as it is defined with respect to the forms of change occurring in the country as a whole. Whereas the stereotypic attributes of a bangsa are inherent and may be considered "racial," even though to the observer they are cultural, there are other stereotypes which are, to the Malay villager, cultural and not inherent. These stereotypes and the processes of change are the subjects of the following chapters.

CHAPTER 2

The previous chapter took as its theme the relationship of villagers to the other races of Malaya, a theme peculiar to Malaya and typical only of those societies described as plural. Village experience has also been affected by events of the outside world as they have manifested themselves in Malaya. Since the village itself is in no sense self-contained, villagers relate to persons outside the village in their various role capacities.

Jendram Hilir is not a social unit within any context of Malay life, except perhaps the imposed unity it has as a religious congregation and as an administrative unit within the mukim. The social relations of the population must, therefore, be referred to criteria other than the territorial. The social horizon of the individual villager is not village-bound but extends to individuals living in other parts of Malaya. In the case of Jendram Hilir, which is located close to such major cities as Seremban, Kajang, and Kuala Lumpur, every-day village experience extends with ease to encompass urban culture. Within the past twenty-five years, the village has been involved in modern warfare waged between the British and Japanese, and between the British and Communist guerrillas. Most recent has been the Confrontation between Malaysia and Indonesia, during which armored

-38-

cars patrolled the village and police road blocks were set up at the entrance to the village. Less tangible evidence of national involvement in world affairs has come from the achievement of Independence, first by Malaya and later by the composite nation, Malaysia. Thus rural experience is not ignorant of the affairs that derive from the consequences of the actions of Western modernity.

At another level of experience, more general and less specific but deriving from the same outside sources, is the guiding and prodding of villagers away from the realm of the traditional illiterate and nonmechanized culture to the alien modernism of the twentieth century. This process began with the assumption of political control by the British in the previous century, when Malays learned to obey government by bureaucracy and code, and has continued to the present time, when it is the Malays who are the bureaucrats, with the villagers the seeds to be cultivated for rural development. Whether they like it or not, village Malays are now caught up in the process of acculturation and modernization. The articulation of villagers into this outside world and their views of it provide the theme for this chapter.

Familiarity with urban life is based on a continuum beginning with the small towns of Bangi and Dengkil, each less than five miles from the village, continuing on to the district capital and commercial center of Kajang, some thirteen miles away, and ending with Kuala Lumpur, the federal capital, and Seremban, capital of Negri Sembilan, each thirty miles from the village. Transportation is no problem, since all towns are served by bus lines and Kuala Lumpur and Seremban can be reached through connections in Kajang. Taxi service is also available, though only occasionally used.

Bangi and Dengkil are within easy cycling distance, and this is the most common means of transportation when men go alone. When women and children go, the bus is used. Both towns have electricity, and many of the appliances and gadgets that go with electricity are found in the homes and stores—lamps, stoves, radios, television, flatirons, refrigerators, and so on. The plan of each town is approximately the same: There is a main street lined with Chinese shops and a Chinese concentration around the center (with a few Indian families who own stores). The Malays live on the edge of the town. Chinese make up about 55 per cent of the population in each town, and Malays comprise about 25 per cent of the population. Both towns have a daily produce market, owned and operated by Chinese and for the most part supplied by Chinese. There is also a weekly market, at which Chinese vendors sell tools, cloth, and utensils, and Malay women sell cakes, fruit, and vegetables. A police station, school, and clinic supply the other public, urban facilities in each town. Bangi, on the main Kuala Lumpur—Singapore railway line, has a rail halt, and Dengkil, the headquarters of the penghulu, has a lumber yard which supplies timber to the surrounding population and possesses Public Works Department labor lines. The main interest of these small towns for villagers is the stores, particularly the rubber-buying stores, the grocery stores, and the pharmacy. The other stores—appliance, stationery, and cloth—are patronized principally by the Chinese population. There are also three coffee shops, owned by a Chinese, an Indian, and a Malay, respectively. Although there are a couple of small Malay stores in each town, villagers do not buy anything from them if they can get it elsewhere. This policy is quite deliberate, because, according to the villagers, the Malay shopkeeper charges too much and will not bargain like the Chinese.

Most of the rubber produced in Jendram Hilir is sold to Chinese buyers in one or the other of these two small towns. Visits to the towns, therefore, are regular. A number of households also purchase a good percentage of their goods at the same time as they sell the rubber—tools, kerosene, flour by the sack, and anything else that occasionally needs replacement but which is neither a daily purchase nor a major purchase. Particular households sell rubber to the same dealer and tend to patronize the same store on each occasion, so that a slightly less formal relationship with the storekeeper is established than if each purchase were conducted at random. The relationship, however, never gets personal and does not approach the relaxed and familiar conduct typical of the village storekeeper and his customers. Contact between villagers and Malays living in either Bangi or Dengkil is minimal. The primary focus of contact between Malays of Jendram Hilir and Dengkil is the penghulu, but relations are wholly formal and concerned only with official business. Two households in Jendram Hilir have kinsmen in Bangi whom they visit periodically, but otherwise there is no social contact.

Contacts between the village and Kajang are more diverse and many-stranded, for Kajang is both the commercial and administrative center of the district of Ulu Langat. In addition, it has a large Malay population, and many villagers have kinsmen living in Kajang. Villagers are drawn to Kajang for supplies and accouterments required on festival and ritual occasions, when a feast (kendury) is to be given, and to make major purchases such as furniture and furnishings, radios, bicycles, and jewelry. Because of the larger selection available, village women also prefer to buy their cloth from Kajang. In contrast to the policy of shopping pursued in Bangi and Dengkil, villagers shop around in Kajang

-41-

to get the best buy, rather than try to build up a special relationship with a particular storekeeper. Since the purchases are infrequent and involve more of an outlay, the multiplicity of stores offers more choice, and variability is evident. The exception is that of the one Chinese trader, noted above, who has managed to more or less corner the village market for radios and bicycles. Although there are three cinemas in Kajang which show up-to-date films, the fact that the last bus leaves for Jendram Hilir at 6 P.M. precludes villagers from seeing too many films there. If they go, it is usually to the matinee. In spite of the presence of cinemas in Dengkil and Bangi, very few villagers go regularly, though if an opportunity for transportation arises (such as the ethnographer's car), it will be quickly snapped up by the young men of the village.

Visits to the district office on official or legal matters are necessary on occasion, but are looked on with trepidation even though the matter may be simple. Similarly, the hospital at Kajang is a place that is feared and avoided, sometimes with unfortunate consequences.* When either of these two places must be visited, villagers attempt to visit a friend or kinsman at the same time, so that the pleasure of a social visit will offset the unpleasantness of an official visit. On the other hand, a visit to one of the two Chinese doctors favored by the villagers is not looked upon in the same way, and a visit to one of them will be combined with a shopping expedition rather than a visit to kin or friends (though not invariably). Very few people in the village hesitate or are afraid to visit the

---

*As when an eleven-year-old boy sustained a fractured arm and broken wrist by falling from a tree and walked around for three weeks with a useless arm which was knitting together crooked. His father was afraid to take him to the hospital and did not realize that a doctor could attend anything other than a sickness or a fever (demam).

doctor, but most prefer to wait a while and see what course their malady
is going to take before they go, since it does mean a journey which, together with the wait, can take up to a whole morning and run to some
expense. In the village there are two bomoh, or medicine "men" (actually, both are women). One claims proficiency only in treating women's
diseases and proceeds to diagnosis and prescription only after going into
a trance. She is very old and infirm and was consulted only once during
my stay. The other makes no pretensions to cure anything much more
severe than a headache, although I was told that she was able to relieve
depression caused by spirit bewitchment (which she herself did not confirm). They are, therefore, consulted only irregularly.

Kajang presents all the appearance of a modern urban center. The
style of life that can be described as "urban" is associated principally
with the Chinese, however, rather than the Malay population, even though
Malay houses are almost as full of electrical appliances as are the Chinese
and a number of Malays own cars or motorcycles. Many Malays live in
Kajang, and a number of villagers regularly visit Malay kin and friends
in Kajang, but the town is considered a different world, one that does
not belong to the Malay. This attitude is evidenced only slightly in the
village opinion of Bangi and Dengkil and, at its most extreme, toward
Kuala Lumpur. Certain features of Malay life in Kajang give an idea of
how this way of thinking can come about.

The Malay population there lives quite separately from the Chinese
and Indian population, who are concentrated about the center of the town.
The Malay sector of Kajang is almost totally independent of this center,
and people do not focus their social life on the town center, but on the
mosque and local coffee shop, thus repeating the village pattern. Houses

-43-

are surrounded by trees and plants and are, in many instances, identical to those found in the village of Jendram. Even though the furnishings are more elaborate and gadgetry more in evidence, they remain more for show than use. Meals are usually eaten seated on the floor, and fingers are used just as in the village. Refrigerators are rarely used for storing foods, but rather for cold drinks and ice cream—to which village Malays are extremely partial. Although a gas stove may occasionally be used, many town houses also use wood or charcoal, and all cook the same food and dishes as village Malays. Whether in town or country, the Malay male changes into a sarong whenever he intends to remain in the house for any length of time, and always spends the evening in the traditional Malay costume, which includes sarong, loose shirt, and songkok (it is mandatory that he pray in these clothes). The Malay woman in village or town, wears the traditional and becoming Malay dress, and very few Malay women have taken to wearing Western (urban) style dresses. The sophisticated accomplishments of urban Malays—their training, literacy, or other skills that keep them working in the towns, are not evident in their domestic lives, except in their use of books in Malay and English, typewriters, record players, etc. Thus the house and the life of the household, the major repositories and anchors of Malay identity, remain only superficially marked by the town. As Sendut (1962: 122) has observed, Malays tend to move into small towns because in many respects they contain features that are not markedly different from those of big villages. One is tempted to go further and suggest that Malays live in villages within towns, and that the significance of this is not so much the existence of any corporate village life but rather the persistence of Malay cultural life centered on the maintenance of the Malay home. Thus when the village

-44-

Malay visits his urban kinsman or friend in Kajang, he sees him only in his domestic role, not in his occupational urban role, and the domestic role and context remains relatively little changed from the village. Conversely, Malay officials of the bureaucracy are never encountered in their domestic roles by the villagers, and they tend to be removed from the realm of Malay culture into the realm of the city: they are orangorang moden to the villagers, who are orangorang kampong. The former are only tenuously Malay, whereas Malay culture, or adat (and therefore real Malay) embraces only orangorang kampong.

This outlook is carried to the limits of generalization with respect to the Malay population of Kuala Lumpur and to the population of Kuala Lumpur in general. Kuala Lumpur is the epitome of the city, and the city is the personification of all that is alien to Malay adat, or what villagers regard as the Malay way of life. The majority of the Malay population of Kuala Lumpur live in kampong (the exclusively Malay settlements within the city), the two most notable being Kampong Baharu, which is located within easy reach of the commercial and business center of the city, and the new Kampong Dato Keramat, which is a government-sponsored development situated on the edge of the city. Another major concentration lives in the new industrial suburb of Petaling Jaya. By comparison with the total population, the Malay inhabitants live in a setting and fashion which approximates the rural kampong and within which the way of life manifests traits that are exclusively Malay. Yet the degree of departure from the norms of kampong life are sufficient to cause the kampong dweller to lump together urban Malays as a subspecies of Malay culture or, for some, especially middle-aged and elderly women, as a semi-detached appendage. One middle-aged lady of Jendram Hilir, when

-45-

expatiating about the town, noted that it was hard to tell Malays and Chinese apart in Kuala Lumpur. It is commonly believed in the village that one of the first things to disappear in the towns is the proper observance of Islam: Malays particularly, like Chinese, take up alcohol, and relax sexual standards. Town Malays, they say, have no time to pray, become over concerned with money, become usurers, and involved in crime. Women sometimes give up wearing Malay dress and lose the gentleness and modesty that they possess in the kampong, so that they can be seen in bars, smoking in public, frequenting coffee shops, and working in dance halls. Malays of the town lose that sensitivity to other people which kampong people prize so highly and become less sensitive to the world around them. The town is characterized as noisy, dirty, smelly, and as simply "no good." Only certain of the younger villagers, particularly the members of the village geng, look with favor on Kuala Lumpur and towns in general. Some of the younger men of the village go off to Seremban for a day or so, where they visit bars (to drink beer) and night clubs. Some of the geng members have also been to the major pleasure palace in Kuala Lumpur—the Bukit Bintang Dance Hall.

This negative opinion of the city and its people derives in part from the fact that the city is equated with the Chinese, so that the stereotype of the city is also the stereotype of the Chinese. Insofar as it is applied to Malays living in the city, it contradicts much of individual village experience, however, which is based in some cases on actual city dwelling and in others on visits and acquaintance with kinsmen living in the city. The Jendram Hilir villagers who have lived in the city at one time or another include eleven men, all over fifty years old, who spent between three and fifteen years living in Kuala Lumpur and, in one case, Ipoh.

Among them there were four commercial drivers, a garage hand, two watchmen, and five coolies who had worked for European- or Chinese-run firms. Unlike many other villages, there are no retired policemen living in Jendram Hilir. Seven of the wives of these men had also lived with them in the city. Two men who lived in the village had worked in cities as watchmen—one in Kajang and the other in Kuala Lumpur. Another man, divorced, lived in Kajang, but returned to the village regularly to visit his mother and his children, who were living with her. Fifteen men had served in the armed forces at one time or another and had gained extra-village experience in this way. Almost every household had kinfolk living in either Seremban, Kajang, or Kuala Lumpur with whom regular contact was kept up. Other kin were also living in Singapore, Ipoh, and Penang. A visit to kin living in Kuala Lumpur is undertaken quite regularly, although there is some variation between households, based largely on wealth differentials. Some idea of frequency of visiting is given in the following table, which covers an eight-month period and includes the festival month of Hari Raya Puasa.

Table 1

Number of visits to kin in Kuala Lumpur	Number of households
5	4
4	11
3	13
2	2
1	3
0	1

With the one exception of a father visiting his son in the hospital, no member of any household visited Kuala Lumpur for any reason other than making a social visit to kinfolk. The visits were usually combined with shopping, however, most frequently for jewelry and cloth, of which Kuala Lumpur offered the most choice and the best prices.* Part of the reason that a trip to Kuala Lumpur must include a visit to kin is that the bus timetable makes a return trip on the same day difficult, so that over-night accommodation is required. But this is only incidental—the major motive is the social visit, a characteristic described more fully below. Social visits to Kuala Lumpur and other towns are returned by kinsmen from the towns, who often arrive on weekends in their own cars or, in the case of some of the younger men, on motor scooters, complete in uniform of black leather jacket and jeans.

The apparent discrepancy between the over-all village stereotype of the town and those who live in it and the individual kinship nature of the ties between villagers and townsmen, from whom village urban experience is derived, is not seen as a contradiction by villagers. No villager regards his town-dwelling kinsman as being permanently settled in the town, but always as spending only a part of his life there for a specific reason—accumulating cash or sending children to school are the principal reasons given. Therefore, no one's kinsmen are "typical" orang bandar, and all will at some time or other return to live in a kampong. For many this will probably be the case, though not for all, and research now being conducted in Kuala Lumpur will reveal more accurately the pattern of urban Malay settlement. For the majority of villagers, however, no one of their acquaintance is really a city person, and the city remains a population alien to the villager. The same reasoning

---

*The difficulty of carrying anything else back to the village limits shopping in Kuala Lumpur.

accompanies individual decisions to live and work in the city, so that kampong dwellers, in spite of their generally negative attitude toward the city, find little difficulty in making the decision to migrate there. They assume that they will not stay in the city for more than a brief period and that they will be living with kin who are of the same mind as they. The transition from the kampong to the city does not require any structural re-alignment of social relations. The household remains the social unit, and the migration of a household or of members of a household from village to town does not rupture any significant social grouping. The dependence of the villagers of Jendram Hilir on a cash income from their rubber and their need to live by cash make the economic transition from kampong to city easy in some ways, although the change in pattern of expenditure had brought on difficulties for a number of families with whom I was acquaint-ed. The increased pressure to own various appliances, the need to antici-pate and budget for utility bills and bus or taxi fares, as well as the greater cost of food all create financial planning problems for town-dwelling Ma-lay families.

The scope of urban experience for some villagers extends as far as Singapore. Members of five households in Jendram Hilir have visited Singapore at one time or other, and three households have close kin liv-ing there. In view of the precarious situation of Singapore, even after its independence, it is of some interest to record Malay village opinion about Singapore. Those villagers who actually lived there lived in Malay kam-pong removed somewhat from the town, and their experiences dated from almost thirty years back. Contemporary notions about the island were shaped by the reports of relatives living there who came to the vil-lage to attend a wedding. In the first place, since Singapore is so

-49-

predominantly Chinese, its way of life and culture is regarded as foreign, but since it was at that time an integral part of Malaysia, and since it is geographically almost inseparable from Malaya, villagers regard it as belonging to the Malays. The visitors from Singapore expounded to a gathering of villagers on life in Singapore, depicting themselves as being a minority oppressed and discriminated against, forced to live in the poorest parts of the island and the city, unable to gain access to good housing, welfare, and other benefits, and steadily being economically strangled by the Chinese. One man, as he warmed to his subject, proceeded to lurid tales of the violence of the Chinese and of their sexual depravity, and told how neither he nor any Malay ever walked abroad without being armed and would go out at night only in groups. It was impossible for a Malay to set up a store in Singapore, because the Chinese would simply rob the store bare. The only solution, the speaker went on, was either the expulsion or the slaughter of the Chinese, and he personally favored the latter course. The hatred of the Chinese that he evidenced was echoed by other members of his family, and the violent course he advocated was looked on with approval by his audience. The juxtaposition of frustration through inferiority with the suggestion of violence as a solution in this Malay's account seems to reflect the more general analyses offered of the riots between Malays and Chinese in Singapore. Although this account of life in Singapore may be inaccurate, its importance here is that this provided first-hand information about Singapore for the villagers, and it is this opinion and outlook that they absorb and use to analyze the general situation as it comes to them over the radio and in newspapers.

Direct experience of other parts of Malaya by people of the village is considerable and derives from the proclivity for visiting and traveling which is typical of many villagers. It is especially associated with women whose children have grown up and, to a slightly less extent, with men of the same status. The word used to describe what is almost a pastime for those who can afford it is jalanjalan, which describes both an evening stroll and the constant tripping around the country to visit friends and relatives and to attend the kendury (celebrations) being held by friends and relatives (often quite distant). The women who make these trips frequently take along a grandchild, both for company, help, and also to show off to their hosts, and in this way many villagers get some idea of other parts of the country. The lines which this visiting follows are usually kin, but friends may also exchange visits, and in many cases the visits are between saudara who have not seen each other for many years. The journeyings of one lady in the village during an eight-month period illustrate the extent of this traveling, although it should be noted that she is somewhat exceptional. She herself is about sixty years of age, a grandmother, illiterate, and from a household with a weekly income averaging (M) $100. She made one trip to Trengganu, where she stayed three weeks with relatives. She visited friends twice in Negri Sembilan, once to attend a funeral, and on both occasions she stayed three days. She made seven trips to various villages in different parts of Selangor to visit kin and friends—in six of these she stayed at least two days and the other overnight. During the festival month of Hari Raya Puasa following Ramadan, she and members of her family made trips constantly. She visited her sister in Petaling Jaya eight times (receiving five visits in return), and she regularly—several times a week—visited people in nearby villages. When she returned from a trip, she informed other members of her family and her friends in the village of the interesting parts of her trip, the health and general situation of the

-51-

people she visited, and any acquaintances of other villagers she met. Then in more general terms she reported on aspects of the area and the village she had visited.

From the answers to questions asked in villages in other parts of Malaya it would appear that such travel is not uncommon. Other writers (Firth 1946; Tjoa 1963) report seasonal migration of Kelantan fishermen to Kedah and other Malay states, although Djamour notes that Singapore Malays "do not like to travel far afield" (1959: 33). The general effect of this travel is to provide villagers with first-hand experience of variations of Malay life and culture, thereby creating an over-all sympathy among all Malays and offsetting to some extent the tenuousness of "Malay" culture. In view of the initiative of women within the context of household life and their general independence, the fact that much of this social traveling is carried out by women is significant, for in itself it comprises part of their independence. It also provides the direct experience that informs their opinions, which in turn may be used in the influencing of decisions and the shaping of attitudes—particularly of children growing up within the household.

The first-hand experience of Indonesia that has been enjoyed by a number of villagers is an important factor in understanding the knowledge of and sympathy with that country as part of the outside world. This is further solidified by the identification and continuity of bangsa within the village and patchwork bangsa organization of the mukim as a whole and, in general, of the western part of Malaya. Thus in a cultural sense, as mentioned in the previous chapter, Indonesia, and Sumatra in particular, are seen as the place of origin, whereas Malaya is culturally (though not politically) a country of adoption. In many senses there is no distinction between the countries—the presence of national political boundaries is to many villagers, especially those with first-hand knowledge of Sumatra, quite artificial. The policy of Confrontation, therefore, was quite incomprehensible to many, and their first-hand experience and indirect cultural sympathies are opposed to any attempt to create a picture of Indonesia as an alien country. The expressed opinions of villagers indicate that their cultural sympathy and empathy with Indonesia are far greater than their ability to identify politically as Malaysians opposed to Indonesians. In this respect the effectiveness of news media in the formation of opinion was comparatively limited, at least during the period of my own field work. News media—especially radio, films, and the printed word—are, however, a major source of knowledge of the outside world.

Fifty-five households in the village have at least one radio, and all households in the village are within earshot of a radio. Although neither coffee shop has a radio, the general store plays one throughout the day, its most regular listeners being the young men of the geng. Radio Malaysia is most often listened to, but Radio Djakarta is heard by most listeners at least once a day, partly for news broadcasts and partly for music. During the time of my field work, the programs of Radio Malaysia were constantly interspersed with patriotic songs and exhortations encouraging Malaysians to oppose Indonesia and to unite as one people. Sample slogans are: "Malaysians will not be crushed," "Malaysia stands united," "Beware the enemies in our midst—Protect Malaysia," "United we stand against evil plans, unity in our own endeavors," and "Malaysia forever." The new national anthem ("Negara Kita") and other songs, many specially composed for the new nation, were repeated throughout the day. Within a few weeks many of the village children knew the words and tunes

of the various songs and sang them with the broadcast. The constant repetition also made many of the adult population familiar with the songs,
but how far the sentiments contained within the songs (sentiments of unity
and patriotism aimed at overcoming the racial diversity of the new nation)
were understood by villagers is difficult to gauge. It can be noted, however, that the radio as a source of information is thought of as being less
authoritative than the written word. Factors which distract from the content of the message are too evident and weigh considerably with villagers.
The accent of announcers, some of whom are thought to be Chinese, the
stilted presentations, and even the content of the programs suggest too
much the urban culture of Malaysia to the villagers. Radio Djakarta, on
the other hand, was said by a number of villagers to be more comprehensible to them, sounding as if the programs were addressed especially to
them. The fleeting character of the spoken word also detracts from its
authority by comparison with the written word. Thus something seen or
read in a newspaper or a magazine is, almost by definition, factual truth
and certainly beyond question by villagers.

No one in the village actually receives a newspaper regularly, although I took it upon myself to supply a copy of the Berita Harian (the
Rumi-script, Malay-language newspaper) and the Utusan Melayu (Jawi
script) to the Malay-owned coffee shop as often as I could. Once in a
while, someone would bring back a newspaper after a shopping expedition
or a visit to one of the small towns. Newspapers are also brought into the
village by visitors. Those who read the newspapers at the coffee shop
read current papers, but most of the reading in the village was of out-of-
date material. Literacy within the village is greater in the Arabic (Jawi)
script than in the Rumi (Roman) script, and the Jawi script Utusan Melayu

is preferred reading. All the men, with the exception of some very old ones, are able to read the Arabic script to some extent, since this is the script of Islam.[*] All newspapers and magazines are avidly read, no matter how out-of-date, and illustrated papers are much preferred. Thus the first items read in a newspaper are the captions to the photographs and other pictures, which are also closely examined. The illustrated advertizements are then scrutinized and are often discussed if they relate to medicine and virility. Only after these have been looked at does the reader start to examine the news articles, of which the human interest stories are first read in full—robberies, items about families, and religious stories. Finally the main news stories are perused. During the course of a week or so, the entire newspaper is likely to be read, but in the beginning, stories are read out loud and the pages are distributed among those drinking coffee. Film magazines, profusely illustrated, are extremely popular whenever they find their way into the village. As previously mentioned, the literature most readily available in the village as a whole are the newspaper pages used for wrapping goods and food bought from the village store and other stores where villagers may shop. This reading matter has already been mentioned. Household calendars and posters also provide information about the outside, but here it should be noted that the effectiveness of propaganda posters is considerably modified by the standard of the art work used. The posters that draw the most attention are those illustrated by well-produced photographs. Posters illustrated by crude drawings and unappealing color (most frequently health posters and

---

[*] Jawi is considered to be superior to Rumi, because it is said to be capable of wider expression, and because it is incomprehensible to non-Malays (i.e. Chinese).

posters encouraging the production of rubber) are never read for the message they are supposed to convey but become the butt of critical comments. Potentially the most important items of reading matter are comic books, which are widely available in stationery stores in the small towns. These are brought into the village by some of the children who attend school in Kajang, by visitors from outside, and by the villagers themselves. Comics are closely read and never thrown away. The stories told in comic books are apparently more easily understood and retained than stories from magazines or other media. The popularity of comic books among all levels of literacy is striking—many students at the University of Malaya can be seen reading comics in the University Library as a break from their more demanding studies.

It has already been mentioned that there are cinemas in the nearby small town of Dengkil and in Kajang, and also that attendance by villagers is limited by the bus schedule. Nevertheless, commercial films are not strange to villagers. Twice during the period of field work a mobile projector from the Information Services visited the village to show films of a propaganda nature. These showings were well attended, but few members of the audience paid much attention to the films, and when, during the break between films the Information Officer delivered his message, many took it as a signal to go for a stroll, or for coffee, or to go home. Since most of the commercial films attended by the villagers are Malay films, they do not serve as a medium of information about the world outside Malaya.

In sum, the most effective sources of information about the outside world for village Malays are their own first-hand experiences through travel—experience gained by the men through seeking work and women through social visiting after they have achieved a senior and independent status. Information passed on by word of mouth describing the experiences or opinions of those with first-hand knowledge is also an influential opinion molder. Of the various forms of news media, the radio is the most permeating and the written word the most authoritative. Although extremely popular, the cinema is inconveniently located for villagers, and its potential influence as a source of information is therefore somewhat limited.

There are certain institutions organized from without the village, with a scope that extends throughout Malaya, which tie in people of the village to the outside (this being the major objective of these institutions). Nationally, the most important of these is the United Malay National Organization (UMNO), which has a cell in Jendram Hilir and in the majority of villages throughout the west coast of Malaya. But whereas in many other villages the UMNO cell is a political rallying point and a ready-made functioning village organization, in Jendram Hilir it barely functions in any capacity at all. This is because the Secretary and guiding spirit is the acting village headman, who belongs to the minority faction in the village and who therefore gains little allegiance from the majority. Instead, the majority rally around the mosque committee as an organization to pursue their own political ends. I was told that the village majority votes UMNO in party contested elections, however, and that at election time the UMNO cell in the village displays some action and solidarity, mainly to impress outside, ranking members of the party. Nevertheless, a comparatively large number of men spoke to me of their sympathies with the Barisan Socialis Party (the Socialist Front).

The Women's Institute is another national organization with cells in each village. Weekly meetings are held in the small, wood and chicken wire hut where cookery (traditional and modern), knitting, hygiene, and other pursuits of feminine interest are studied. In Jendram Hilir the activity of this organization tends to be half-hearted, depending on the energies of three women (whereas in other neighboring villages the Women's Institute is very active). The leading spirit is often the local schoolteacher or the wife of the schoolteacher, but both teachers in Jendram Hilir were recent arrivals, and neither of the two wives was particularly pleased at having to live in the village. Outside speakers and demonstrators occasionally visit the village organization.

Confrontation with Indonesia led to the formation of a nationwide, village-based Vigilante Corps, or Home Guard. The function of this group was primarily to maintain a lookout in each village so that infiltration of guerrillas might be forestalled and the police and army notified in case of trouble. Local organization was undertaken by the penghulu, working through village headmen, and lookouts patrolled the village at night and had their headquarters in the village hall. Eventually they were supplied with five-foot wooden staves, lamps, raincoats, and whistles. From reports in the newspapers and from my own tours of the mukim, it appears that in general the Vigilante Corps was a successful innovation and that it proved effective in its allotted tasks. In Jendram Hilir, however, the patrols functioned only on occasion, since few of the men were willing to participate, and since those who did preferred to spend most of their watch in the village hall (balai rayat), talking and playing cards. This is also an indication of one of the hidden successes of the Corps—the increased feeling of solidarity among members of a village and an increase in their awareness of being members of a larger, political community. This was particularly applicable in small towns such as Bangi and Dengkil, where the watches were, to some extent though not completely, interracial. Although Confrontation had about it an air of unreality to everyone in the country, and to villagers in particular, it served perhaps better than any other factor at the time to involve villagers in the new nationalism.

Of all the influences leading to change in traditional outlook, education is the most significant and most consciously oriented, a fact well recognized by the national government of Malaysia, which is achieving a most impressive school system. Jendram Hilir has a <u>sekolah kebangsaan</u> (primary school), with an enrollment of 114 and a staff of two, and an adult education program which meets once a week with a registration of 65 illiterate adults (40 women and 25 men). Average attendance in the latter program was, however, between six and fourteen. The majority of these illiterate adults are over forty-five years of age and many, both men and women, can read the Arabic script to some extent. Instruction is in the Roman (Rumi) script and includes elementary arithmetic. If it is noted that the illiterate population of Jendram are senior members of the households, responsible for the raising of children within the village, then the significance of their role in modernization can be appreciated. By contrast, although there are many people who were born in the village who have achieved a comparatively high standard of education, they no longer live in the village, but have moved elsewhere to undertake employment more suited to their qualifications. Only the schoolteachers, the storekeeper, one ex-schoolteacher, the <u>imam</u> (head of the mosque), and five other individuals have achieved secondary or advanced schooling and still reside in the village. Many of those who remain in the village have not had the opportunity for a modern education, but at least as many who remain do not have the ability to achieve a higher standard under existing conditions. The majority of the adult population of the village, therefore, has little experience or ability in "modernization," yet it is precisely these people who raise and train the new generation.

The traditional socialization of the home is to some extent, in theory at least, counterbalanced by the existence of the sekolah kebangsaan. But the student/teacher ratio itself gives a clue to the relative inefficiency of the school. Even though the curriculum—on paper—is a most encouraging one, moving toward a Malaysian interpretation of modernization, many of its provisions are difficult to follow. There is no school garden, for example, where children might learn adequate methods of cultivation, although this is required by the national curriculum. Hygiene is learned, like everything else, by mechanical repetition of the precepts, which continue to exist as mere words and are not translated into village life. The question of the effective translation of what is learned through the medium of the written and spoken word and through pictures into the action of everyday life is not one that can be dealt with at this point, though preliminary questioning of children has led me to suspect that the applicability of abstract learning in the classroom to the practical life of the village is not easily effected. The problem, as it appears in Jendram Hilir, may be framed as follows. Each child of the village is subjected to two systems of education. One, the school system, is organized from the outside, is conducted by schoolteachers who are not of the village, and is based on a curriculum using methods of communication and content matter derived from Western culture. It is aimed at educating children toward a proficiency in skills and thought that will be matured, and made relevant to the conduct of life, in schools more advanced than the primary school

-60-

of the village. The second system is that based on the home, where the curriculum includes the arts of life as it is to be lived in the village. These arts—from cooking and hygiene to rubber tapping—are learned directly through participation and observation rather than through the printed word and picture. The first system is linked to aspects of an alien culture, whereas the second is entirely part and parcel of an on-going, locally sanctioned process. In the one system, instruction is impersonal and en masse, whereas in the second system, it is highly personal and individual. Schoolteachers tend to be out of sympathy with village life, whereas the instructors in the home are inextricably bound up with what they teach. Such points are obvious, but it is significant that when the total educational process is considered with respect to "rural development," the system that is perpetuated and taught most efficiently is that which maintains the level characterized as "undeveloped."

It might be suggested, perhaps more as a basis for further research than as any sort of recommendation, that the curriculum and methods of instruction in village primary schools be devised as a direct means of influencing traditional village life, and not thought of as part of a total educational system involving levels of education and methods linked to an alien culture. That is to say, the curriculum should be based on the application of Western, or developmental, concepts to traditional village or rural life. For example, rural development requires modernization of agricultural techniques, including mechanization. Notoriously, abuse of machinery introduced into a rural economy has been contributory to the retardation of development. But one of the hidden assumptions of the culture from which the machinery came is that machinery requires preventive maintenance. In the village of Jendram Hilir, for example, three men who own motor scooters ran them until they ceased to function—they never added or replaced oil, checked plugs or tires, and so forth. No one in the village ever oiled a bicycle or was even capable of effecting a repair beyond mending a puncture. The same ignorance of principles underlies the failure of villagers to keep rubber smallholdings properly cleared of lalang, or weeds. Learning the principles of preventive maintenance with respect to village life, and especially to changing village life, is surely a necessary part of educational development.

To continue this digression, in the teaching of elementary arithmetic in the village school, even though familiar symbols are used (six water buffalo and three water buffalo make nine water buffalo), still the relationship of Western arithmetic to everyday life with respect to development is nowhere present. An example of what I mean can easily be given. As will be mentioned elsewhere, Malay village budgeting is a short-term affair and the village view of all phases of the economic process tends to be a short view (a factor noted by others, e. g. Swift 1965). The inability to amass capital to undertake projects such as replanting is an important factor in the underdevelopment of the Malay rural population. But the conceptual complex of capital and investment, which a Westerner assimilates more or less unconsciously as part of the socialization process, is never conveyed to the Malay as part of his early education. Through devices such as the piggy bank, pocket money, and savings accounts, the Western child understands a number of principles basic to capitalist economy— even though individuals may not always apply them successfully. A primary school curriculum which attempts to explain these concepts and principles of the life toward which change is aimed, and which is oriented toward rural, rather than urban, culture, may well be more productive of

-62-

rural development than many schemes of modernization. Observations as to the methods of conveying such information, although highly preliminary and in dire need of fuller amplification, suggest to me that the media and the symbols used are less effective than a number of possible alternatives. For example, elementary textbooks at best tell a story in which the text is illustrated by pictures. The ease with which villagers follow and assimilate comics suggests that the text and the picture should both tell the same story—that in fact textbooks in the form of comics may be more effective than mere illustrated texts. In trying to explain an airplane to village children, I attempted first to use pictures and words but met with little understanding. But the use of a cheap elastic-driven model enabled me to explain to the children's comprehension the principles by which an airplane flies. Using a model car, I attempted to explain the principles by which an automobile is propelled and why it needs maintenance—a task far more easily accomplished than if words and pictures only were used. It may be noted that visual aids (whether models or the actual objects) are the principal teaching aids used in the education given in the Malay village home.

Returning from this digression to consider the school as a source of information about the outside world, it is indeed a major source of such information, but it has a surprisingly small influence on the knowledge and understanding of the outside world insofar as children and adults of the village are concerned. In part, this may be because neither of the two schoolmasters teaching in the school has yet established a reputation in the village, so that what they have to say, even within the class room, is not necessarily accepted as being so. Also, it may derive from the hiatus between learning in the school and life as it is lived in the village.

The continuity in education is aimed at the progression from primary to secondary and further education rather than from school to village life. Education as a process of qualification for fulfilling newly acquired ambitions is highly approved of by most villagers, who want their children to get the education that will qualify them for jobs in the government bureaucracy and civil service. Consequently, many village children have achieved a secondary education, taken urban-based jobs, and left the village. Six children are currently attending the secondary school in Kajang, and probably more would attend if their parents could afford it and if there were more places available.

Islam is the major institution that not only draws Malays together in sympathy but also unites Malays to peoples of other parts of the world and to a system of thought and behavior located above and beyond any specific culture. Villagers are instructed in the teachings of Islam and in the reading of the Koran from an early age, both in the home and in small religious schools run by local guru. Islam and the learning of Islam are seen as integral parts of the life and being of a Malay, and from the beginning the extra-Malay factors also become familiar—particularly Arabic script and literature and the pilgrimage to Mecca. For many in the village, the limit of what is meaningful in the outside world is Mecca. Those who have made the haj are often called on to describe their travels, and they will often do so even without invitation. Most bring back souvenirs of their visit (usually pictures, a prayer mat, or cloth), and their experience is therefore passed on to others. This involvement with Islam cannot be said to constitute a force or means by which the horizon of the villager of Jendram Hilir is broadened to bring about a self image of being a member of a wider society. Islam is too integral a part of Malay culture for it to be a force for change and new involvement. Even though the pilgrimage takes Malays from their village, it does not lead them out into the world at large. Such events as the annual national Koran-reading competition, which begins with competitors from villages within a <u>waliah</u> (religious district) and ends with State winners competing in the National Stadium in Kuala Lumpur, cannot be said to draw villagers beyond their traditional horizons. The national and international Koran-reading contests arouse great interest in the village, and most households follow the events very closely as they are broadcast over the radio, listening well into the early hours of the morning.

The aim of this chapter and of the previous chapter has been to specify the nature and extent of contact with non-Malay culture by Malay villagers and to try and indicate how villagers evaluate and react to these outside elements. This outside world consists of people—principally Chinese and Indians, but also other Malays—and processes involving principles and artifacts. Jendram Hilir is in no sense an isolated community, but in many ways its people are an insulated community. They are familiar with non-Malay culture, they may even participate in it, but they have not synthesized it so that all facets of their own lives—cultural, social, economic, and religious—cohere into a satisfactory whole. In no way does this seem better illustrated than in the villagers' own consciousness of their increasing cultural anonymity, which is demonstrated in their awareness of the decay of <u>adat</u> customs without any satisfactory substitute. Thus no one in the village now plays a musical instrument, although there are at least eighteen persons who "used to play." With the advent of the radio they no longer have an audience interested in listening, and no longer deem it even enjoyable to play for their own amusement. Yet their shame-faced admission and regret at the condition underline the pathos of the over-all situation. Of the six men in the village who professed themselves capable of doing some of the traditional wood carving, only one old man still does any carving, principally for his own amusement (although he will carve a parang handle and sheath if someone asks him). Of the four men who said they could build a canoe, only two had actually done so within the past twenty years, and only one man, a young ex-schoolteacher who had left teaching because he preferred village life, said that he would continue to build canoes if he or anyone else needed them. The weaving of mats and baskets is a skill common among Malay women, and all the women over forty years old in the village admitted that they knew how to plait, but of these only one still does so. One young woman (the daughter of the woodcarver mentioned above) had learned to weave and regularly uses this skill. Fishing traps and baskets were formerly made in the village and never bought from outside. Today, although the same people who used to make them still live there, only six households make fishing traps and baskets, mainly for their own use, and no one makes nets any more. Such equipment, as well as mats and baskets, are purchased from Chinese merchants and artisans. Probably the only craft still predominantly village-based is dress making— the majority of women make their own dresses or have them made by a member of their own household. But the men's clothing and some children's clothing is store-bought.

Perhaps the most pathetic event illustrating this whole process of the decay of adat customs occurred during a wedding in the village. After the ceremony it came time for the dancing—music for which was provided by a quartet from a village some distance away. The dance in question was the bersilat—derived from traditional Malay fencing. First one man stood and made a few motions, then gave up with a mixture of shame and amusement. He was followed by another who, although somewhat better, was plainly very rusty. The occasion was turned into a joke at which some of the men clowned to cover up the embarrassing situation—there being a number of outsiders present. Although the quartet played throughout the late afternoon, no one danced. Nor during my stay was there evidence of any accomplishment having been acquired that would fill the cultural gap left by this atrophy.

The social and economic expressions of this change are indicated in the relevant chapters.

CHAPTER 3

The process of colonization and economic development of Malaya
by the British led directly, over the course of time, to the establishment
of economic specialization based on ethnic grouping. Chinese laborers
were brought in to work the tin mines and then to provide the particular
needs of the growing Chinese community. Indian labor came in to work
the agricultural estates and plantations and to provide manual labor for
government projects. The Malays showed a preference for remaining on
the land and were encouraged to do so, but they became increasingly dependent on subsistence production as other sources of revenue, such as
taxes and royalties, were reduced and made otherwise inadequate and the
demands of the Chinese markets for food fast outstripped the Malay ability
to supply. Even with the burgeoning of rubber as a cash crop, Malays preferred to raise trees on their smallholdings rather than supply labor to estates or set up their own plantations. The rapid development of a national Malayan economy based on trade with world markets and founded on
tin and rubber not only tended to solidify the economic roles of ethnic
groups but also allowed the Chinese especially to assume initiative and

control, albeit within a framework of British capitalism.[*] With Malays tied to the land and contributing to the cash economy only as primary producers on a small scale, they have, as a whole, become more or less an appendage to the national economy. That the general identification of ethnic groups with economic roles is still well defined may be seen from the following figures: Over 83 per cent of Malay males and 90 per cent of Malay females are engaged in agriculture, forestry, hunting, or fishing. The Chinese population is divided as follows: 29 per cent in commerce, 21 per cent in producing agricultural products requiring proc- essing, 14 per cent in service occupations, 12 per cent in manufacturing, 11 per cent in agriculture, forestry, hunting, or fishing, and 4 per cent in construction, including mining and quarrying. Indians are predomi- nantly (39 per cent) employed in producing agricultural products requir- ing processing (chiefly rubber), 26 per cent are in services, 19 per cent in commerce, and 8 per cent in transportation, storage, and communica- tion (source: Federation of Malaya, Report on Employment, Unemploy- ment and Underemployment, Kuala Lumpur 1962).

The confinement of Malays to the rural sector of the economy and the comparative impoverishment of that sector have been the subject of many studies (e.g. Fisk 1963; Aziz 1964) and an increasing amount of government legislation. The theme is constant: namely to raise the liv- ing standards of the rural, hence Malay, population in order to achieve some form of balance between race, political representation, and eco- nomic potency in a newly independent nation. As a leading economic ex- pert on Malay affairs has stated:

---

[*]A fascinating and brilliant analysis of the structure of Malayan econ- omy is given by Puthucheary, 1960.

This racial division between the advanced and backward sector is of great importance because in political power the rural Malays are the dominant factor,
whilst the political power of the rural Chinese and Indians is relatively smaller, and that of the foreigner
virtually nil. This means that in the formation of any
policy for rural development a responsible Malayan
government must give at least as much attention to the
effect of its policies on the welfare of the participants
of the backward sector as to the effects on the general
level of economic activity of the country as a whole
[Fisk 1963: 163].

At the risk of oversimplification, it may be stated that studies of Malay
economy have been conducted by statistical survey and have paid relatively little attention to Malay values and attitudes concerning economic
affairs (notable exceptions are Firth 1946 and Swift 1965).

The aim of this chapter, therefore, is to attempt a clarification of
Malay village attitudes and values with respect to economic activity. The
major contention is that the social aspects of economic activities are as
relevant and meaningful as aspects that can be reckoned statistically.

The rural sector of the Malayan economy undertaken by Malays may
be divided conveniently into three main segments: padi growing, rubber
tapping, and fishing. Less widespread, though important in many parts,
are fruit growing and coconut/copra production. Although padi is grown
in every state, it is of major economic importance in Kedah, Perak,
Penang, Perlis, Kelantan, and Trengganu. Fishing is important in all
coastal areas, but particularly to the coastal Malays of Kelantan and
Trengganu. Rubber tapping is the major economic product of Malays in
Selangor, Negri Sembilan, Malacca, Johore, Perak, and Pahang, but it is
also grown in all other states.

Of the three segments, rubber tapping is most closely tied into the national economy because it is Malaya's major export and, unlike padi or fish, is not a food crop. All Malays dependent on rubber growing are fully enmeshed in a cash economy, and their dependence on the soil for subsistence is indirect. Since the Malays produce only the raw rubber, which is but one process in the economics of rubber, they are totally dependent on the Chinese, who not only supply cash in exchange for the rubber but also the food and goods that are bought with the cash. Although the quick turnover and nonseasonal basis of rubber production does not lead to the protracted indebtedness incurred by padi-growing Malays, it places the Malay in a most vulnerable position with respect to the Chinese who buy, process, and transport the rubber. Other factors beyond the reach of Malay rubber producers affect the economics of rubber—and hence the living standards of the rural Malay. These include the tie-in of rubber to a world market and its government by world prices and the competition of large, efficiently-run rubber estates (in 1963 estate rubber production was 455,000 tons and smallholding production 329,000 tons). The problems raised by world conditions (competition from synthetics and improvements in rubber yields and quality, for example) can be met by estates through controlled replanting and experiments. Malay smallholders have neither the resources nor the inclination to move with such changes. Another problem, illustrated particularly in the village here studied but of widespread import, is that the trees on many Malay smallholdings are coming to the end of their productive lives. Since rubber trees do not yield until about seven years after planting, the Malay smallholder must find another way to secure an income in the interim.

The day-to-day life of Malay villagers is bound up with the tapping and preparation of rubber and I now turn to a detailed examination of rubber production and the domestic economy in the village of Jendram Hilir. When trees are in yield, usually when they are between the ages of seven and forty years, they can be tapped throughout the year and are not subject to seasonal conditions. However, latex (susu) does not run properly following rain, so rubber production falls off during the rainy season.

The daily pattern, uniform throughout the village, begins at about 5:00 A.M. or anytime within two hours after that, when the tapper leaves the house for the trees he intends to tap that day. He visits each tree in turn, to adjust or place the cup that receives the latex, which runs down the groove cut with a knife in a special pattern in the bark of the tree. The time this takes depends on the number of trees to be tapped and on whether the trees are old or not, since old trees are usually tapped higher up on the trunk, which requires the tapper to climb a ladder. As the heat of the day increases, the flow of the latex slows down and after three to four hours ceases, having produced about a cupful, which is emptied into a large tin can. The overflow and dribbles from the incision collect at the bottom of the tree, and these too are collected after they have coagulated. These rubber hunks are termed getah buku and are sold at a lower price than the latex.

While the latex is flowing, the tapper either returns to his house, where he may take coffee or, if the walk is too lengthy (very often tappers cycle to a distant holding) he remains in the holding (kebon), where he may doze or gossip with a neighbor. Having collected the latex in the cans, he then takes it to the tempat getah for processing. The tempat getah comprises a floor space with a roof, a raised table area, and two types of mangle—one with smooth rollers and the other with grooved. It is always located near water, to facilitate cleaning of cans and tools, but sometimes the tempat getah is situated in the kebon and sometimes back in the yard of the house in the village. Here the latex is poured into large shallow pans something like baking dishes and coagulated by the addition of formic acid. It is stirred, turned out, flattened on the floor area, and then wrung out several times into a sheet (keping) measuring approximately three feet by eighteen inches and weighing between two and four kati (kati - 1 1/3 pounds). The keping are then either hung out over a pole to dry in the sun or laid out on the ground. The quality of the rubber would be considerably improved by smoking, but there is no smokehouse in the village (very few villages possess one), so that at best the rubber is sold reasonably dry. The daily round is completed between noon and 2:00 P.M. Few tappers work more than five days a week, and only one quite exceptional household actually works a regular five-day week.

All phases of tapping are carried out by men, women, and children. Even the heaviest tasks of collecting and carrying are done by women as well as men. But when men and women work together, there is some tendency for the men to collect and carry and for the women to take over at the tempat getah. Except in the case of a woman living without a man, men do all the selling of rubber, carrying the sheets on the back of a bicycle or going to the dealers by bus. Rarely, because it works so rarely, is the village car used to transport rubber to Bangi or Dengkil. There is a rubber buyer in Jendram, a former ketua kampong who acts as an agent for a Chinese merchant in Kajang. But since the price paid in Jendram is six cents a kati less than elsewhere, villagers sell only under specific circumstances (see below).

Another demanding task is the control of scrub and weeds (lalang)

-73-

that can easily overrun a smallholding. With the exception of a minority
of holdings, most are choked out with undergrowth, and the majority of
holders rarely make more than one attempt a year at clearing out the
scrub. This reduces the yield of the trees growing there. Although holdings planted within the past twenty years or so have the trees spaced out
and in rows, the majority of holdings, which were planted nearly forty
years ago, have trees scattered more or less at random.

The tools and equipment necessary for rubber tapping are relatively
simple and inexpensive, except for the mangles. A specially shaped
knife is used to make the groove in the bark down which the latex runs,
porcelain or plastic cups are held to the trunk by wire, and metal suku,
or spouts from which the latex drips into the cup, are required (the suku
is often a folded leaf). Cans, mixing pans, formic acid, a stirring spoon,
and the mangles are required for preparing the latex. All these, except
the mangles, are made locally by Chinese artisans out of tin sheeting and
discarded paint cans. Only the formic acid, at (M) 50 cents for a week's
supply, must be regularly purchased, otherwise the outlay on tools is between $5-$10 (Malay) depending on quantity of tins bought. Seventeen
households in the village own mangles, and these are rented out at a standard rate of (M) $1.00 a month.

Of the 108 households functioning in the village during the time of
field work, 88 owned rubber holdings, or had direct access to holdings
owned by an absentee relative. Twenty households had no land at all.
The distribution of acreage of rubber land among households is given in
the accompanying table (see following page).

A total of 490 acres is planted with rubber and owned by village
members, an average of approximately 4.5 acres per household. The

-74-

Table 2. Rubber Acreage per Household

Rubber acreage	Number of households
0	20
0. 1-3	28
3. 1-6	32
6. 1-9	15
9. 1-12	6
12. 1-15	4
15. 1-18	2
18. 1-21	1
	108

holdings of many households are split up into parcels located at various places around the village, although most households have at least one holding near the house. Eleven households have holdings which now produce little or no rubber because of age of the trees and poor state of the holding. These households, and the nonlandowning households rent land, and their members work as "coolies" for other holders. The exact details of ownership, title, and inheritance of land must unfortunately be omitted, since I was unable to collect sufficient accurate data in the time at my disposal. A few general observations should suffice. There had been much buying and selling of land in the past, but this is now considerably reduced. The majority of the buyers were villagers who had left the village and who live and work in towns such as Kajang and Kuala Lumpur as civil servants and schoolteachers. Kinsmen look after the holdings, tap them, and in return receive a fraction of the income. In many cases, holdings presently being tapped have been inherited and the division of an individual's holdings into parcels is a result of the fragmentation brought about by the division of land among the heirs and by individuals planting their own holdings where land is available to supplement their inheritance.* Again, clearing of new holdings has now ceased. The area in which Jendram Hilir is located has been set aside as a Malay reservation, and I could find no evidence that any Chinese had any indirect control over the holdings of a Malay villager. Nor did anyone in the village ever rent land to a Chinese, although there are two small Chinese estates on the boundaries of the village. Some villagers mentioned that in the past there had been a number of quarrels and litigation over land, but there had been no recent case. In brief, the over-all picture is one of relative stability in land ownership, but a stability marked by gradual decay in productivity.

The process of rubber tapping and the ownership of land are both focused on the household. There is no cooperation among villagers from different households, but the personnel of a household often form a team. The only time different tapping teams come together is at the tempat getah, where people await their turns for use of the mangles. If the users of a tempat getah are close kinsmen (keluarga) or friends (kawan), this coming together at the tempat getah is often a time of gossip and joking. Otherwise, teams have little to say to each other, and simply get on with rolling the keping. Only in the cases where a rubber holder uses coolies to tap for him is there any extension of relationships outside the household. This relationship, which will be described below, is more than just an economic one and has distinct social overtones. The households employing coolie labor (the term "coolie" is used in the village) own an average of thirteen acres. Of these larger smallholders, seven are elderly and do no

---

*Rubber holdings are not thought of as traditional (adat) property subject to disposal only by inheritance (harta pusaka). They are bought and sold.

tapping themselves, although they usually sell the rubber themselves.
Fifty-two individuals from twenty-two households work regularly as coolies
for others in the village, and in so doing are established in a relationship
termed tolong menolong. The term is derived from the view of the nature of the work performed—i. e. the relation between landowner and
coolie is idealized as being a reciprocal relation between equals, rather
than an employment relation between unequals. Alternatively, the system
of coolie labor is called bagi dua, a term derived from the fact that the
coolie and the landowner each receive half of the proceeds from the sale
of the rubber. The sheets produced by each coolie are specially marked
by inserting a patterned stencil in the mangle when they are being rolled,
and they are usually stored separately.

Rubber tapping is the major productive activity of all households in
the village. It requires little equipment or initial outlay, since many of
the trees were planted by ancestors of the present tappers. The entire
process employs the household as the largest production unit, but in many
cases the complete cycle can be, and often is, carried out by individuals.
There are no seasonal restrictions, and the cycle is complete in one day
(although it is preferable for the sheets to be allowed to dry for at least a
week). The standard of living that rubber tapping affords in the village
and the working habits of households may be indicated by details from a
sample of ten households studied over a one-week period, supplemented
by general observations of all households in the village made during the
period of field work. The sample week, during November, was rainless,
and there were no ritual celebrations, so no time was lost because of outside happenstance.

The ten households worked a total of 599 man hours, an average of

33. 33 hours per week per person, or 4.75 hours per day. Eleven of the 18 people worked less than the average (i.e. seven of the ten households). Only one household, consisting of three working adults, averaged a six-hour workday. Those tapping their own trees averaged 39 hours per week per person and those working as coolies averaged only 15.6 hours per week per person. The entire sample is heavily weighted by two households, one owning its own land and working an average of 55 hours a week, and the other a coolie household averaging a 41-hour working week. It must be concluded that the hours put in are far from a reasonable and expectable maximum, which in turn leads to a conclusion that villagers tap only to earn as much cash as they need immediately. During the sample week, three of the male tappers went on overnight fishing trips, and two women spent some time in their vegetable gardens. Otherwise, no one engaged in any other productive activity. A larger sample might yield a more bal-anced picture, but on the other hand, there is no reason to believe that the present sample is distorted.

The price paid by rubber dealers in Bangi, Dengkil, and Kajang is 58 cents per kati for keping getah puteh—i.e. rolled, dried, unsmoked sheets—and between 22 and 25 cents a kati for getah buku—the unprepared left-over rubber collected from the base of the trees. The price for keping getah puteh in Jendram Hilir is 52 cents a kati. A single keping weighs be-tween two and four kati. The agent in Jendram Hilir does not pay cash immediately on receipt of the rubber, but pays once a week when the Chi-nese towkay comes from Kajang to collect the rubber after weighing it. He pays the agent 55 cents a kati, and the agent then pays the tappers. Buyers in Bangi and Dengkil pay immediately on receipt of the rubber. Because it involves a journey of about five miles, and because the amount

-78-

that can be carried on the back of a bicycle is limited, it is not convenient to make trips to Bangi or Dengkil more than once or twice a week,
hence many sell their rubber in the village. The village agent will buy
it wet and hang it out to dry, so that rubber tapped and rolled can be sold
on the same day in the village. This is advantageous to those whose rubber production is small and who plan their activity only on the basis of the
day's needs. The village agent and the storekeeper have an agreement
that allows the former to hand over cash from a tapper's income to pay
off debts accumulated at the store, an arrangement also suitable to tappers. Those with more land and trees can accumulate a stock of rubber,
most of which can be seen or, more accurately, smelled as it hangs above
the hearth in the kitchen or is piled up in the corner of a room or beneath
the house. Such households sell their rubber in Bangi or Dengkil for higher
prices, while the poorer households with less rubber tend to sell their rubber in Jendram Hilir at the lower price.

The majority of villagers do not consider themselves to be poor,
although they subscribe to the generalization that all orangorang kampong
are poor and lack money. The comparison here is with Chinese and Europeans. Even so, within the village there is some differentiation between
orangorang miskin (poor people) and orangorang kaya (rich people), with
the majority of villagers belonging to neither extreme. The poor families are those without land and those who work as coolies. The majority
of these were not born in the village, and some are of the minority bangsa
(mainly the Banjarese). The wealthy households are those with ten or
more acres of land and with cash income from outside (pensions, school-
teaching, and property holdings elsewhere). Households with additional
sources of income also include: a coffee shop owner, two households in

which one member works as a watchman, two storekeepers, the rubber dealer, two agents for Chinese merchants who work in Jendram Ulu, eleven households with wives who receive some income from property held in Negri Sembilan, and one household in which the owner has substantial savings accumulated during his working years. The two schoolmasters, who reside in the village are not from the village, and actually spend their money elsewhere. One woman earns some money and kind acting as a traditional midwife (bidan), and two women make a minute income from practicing as bomoh.

The range of household incomes is from $1.00 to about $50.00[*] a day, and the general pattern of work and income may be gathered from Table 3, which gives figures for a sample of ten households. It might be noted that in computing an annual income, work is affected by the social and religious calendar as well as by rain. Swift (1965: 55) notes that "twenty tapping days a month is regarded as a reasonable working month" and, though no one in Jendram Hilir seemed to have such a specific view of the matter, this probably approximates an acceptable average. (Using the present sample, the average number of working days is seventeen.)

The average daily income for the ten sample households is $5.49, but if household No. 4 is omitted, as it is so plainly exceptional, the average is $3.56. The average weekly income is $38.43, and the average monthly income $153.72. Omitting household No. 4, these figures would read: weekly average $24.92 and monthly average $99.68. In answer to an on-the-spot question, members of 70 households indicated that they thought their average weekly income was between $20 and $30 (average of replies was $24, median $21).

----

[*]All currency in Malay dollars.

-80-

TABLE 3. HOUSEHOLD ECONOMICS

Household	No. in household	No. of workers	Acres of rubber	Hours worked per day							Keping produced per day							Income per day ($ Malay)‡							Total† ($ Malay)	Expenditure ($ Malay)
				1	2	3	4	5	6	7	1	2	3	4	5	6	7	1	2	3	4	5	6	7		
1	5	3	2	6	16	5			24		3	5	2			5		5.22	8.70	3.48			8.70		26.10	19.55
2	6	1			8	6	6			8		3	3	2		3	3		5.22	5.22	3.48			5.22	19.14°	19.63
3	8	1	5	5	6	6	3		8	4	2	2	3	2		3	2	3.48	3.48	5.22	3.48		5.22	3.48	24.36	22.35
4	6	4	16.3	27	24	24	21		26	24	17	16	15	18		13	13	29.58	27.84	26.10	31.32		22.62	22.62	160.08	75.75
5	7	2	6.4	12			8		16	16	3			3		3	2	5.22			5.22		5.22	3.48	19.14	19.75
6	5	3		14	27	27			16	16	6	7	5			8	6	10.44	12.18	8.70			13.92	10.44	18.56†	22.00
7	7	1	3	4	4	8	4			8	2	2	2	2			3	3.48	3.48	3.48	3.48				10.44°	12.05
8	4	1	4.2			6	4			8			3	2			3			5.22	3.48			5.22	13.92°	34.34
9	7	2	13.1		12	12	12		12	12		7	5	7		7			12.18	8.70	12.18		12.18		45.24	29.10
10	2	1				3	4	4	12	4			1	2	1		2			1.74	3.48	1.74		3.48	10.44	?

* A slight overestimate, as some *keping* were sold in the village at 52 cents a *kati.*

† This figure represents one-third of the total earned, as explained on page 85.

‡ Figures calculated from average weight of *keping* (3 *kati*) at 58 cents a *kati.*

Other occasional sources of income available to village households, though not represented in the ten-household sample, are the sale of fruits (especially durian, mango, rambutan, langsat, and mangosteen) at the roadside, and carpentry, at which a number of men were skilled or semi-skilled and very occasionally did some minor house repairs (including mending atap roofs). In addition, there is the one old man who makes parang handles and sheaths, more as a hobby than an occupation. Households with supplements in kind to their regular incomes include: those households with ladang or dry-rice acreage (see below); households with kitchen and vegetable gardens (including one man who gardens full time and depends on this for his living); households with personnel who fish either in the rivers (men) or the ponds and rice fields (women and children). Two households in the village keep herds of goats, numbering roughly thirty at any one time. These are sold on order, but usually outside of the village, to Malays about to celebrate with a feast, or to the meat market in Kajang.

Patterns of expenditure vary little in the village, but the calculation of expenditures is subject to the level of income of the household. Households with an income of $20 a week or more generally have enough cash on hand to be able to meet daily expenses, while those with an income of less than $20 a week often have to live on short-term credit and occasionally have to borrow. Households with an above-average income tend not to budget in detail for each day, but rather to buy what they need when they need it. Poorer households, however, often plan their work for the following day on the basis of what the wife calculates she is going to need in the way of food and supplies. Certain items such as flour, kerosene, and rice are bought by some households at the wholesale price, but most households in the village cannot afford such an outlay at any one time. Some idea of the daily needs and expenses of a household is given in the following summary of the weekly budgets of the sample of ten households for whom working hours and income have already been detailed.

1. The household comprises a man, his mother, his wife, and two small children. The three adults tap rubber, although the two women do not tap each day. The man owns two acres of rubber holding and supplements his income by working as a coolie for a kinsman on an average of two days a week. The income for the week was $26.10 from a working week of 51 man hours. Total expenses for the week came to $19.55, of which $11.98 went for food and kitchen needs, $4.20 for cigarettes and the coffee shop, and the remainder, $3.37, was spent on patent medicine, formic acid, candy, and ice cream (the latter bought from a Malay vendor who visits the village daily from Kajang). The balance for the week was $6.55.

2. The household comprises a man, aged about 64, his wife (about 40), and their four young children. They have no land, having settled in the village about five years ago. The man owns four cows, which he tends most of the day, and he tries to do odd jobs for people if and when he can. The wife, who has kinsmen in the village, works as a coolie and sometimes her husband takes over for her. The eldest boy, eleven years old, sometimes tends the cows and helps his mother tapping. Their income was $19.14 earned from working 28 hours on four days of the week. Expenses were: food, $14.36; cigarettes and betel supplies, $1.80; coffee shop and ice cream, 40 cents; and rent for the use of land to pasture the cows, 25 cents. Total expenditure was $16.81, a balance of $2.33. The family lived rent-free in a house belonging to a kinsman of the wife living elsewhere.

-83-

3. The household comprises a man, his wife, and their six children, one of whom is deaf and dumb. They own five acres of rubber holding. Working a total of 32 man hours on six days of the week, the income was $24.36. Expenses included: $15.15, food and household supplies; $4.70 cigarettes, coffee shop, candy and ice cream; $1.00 as their weekly payment on a transistor radio; and $1.50 a week on a bicycle. Total expenses were $22.35, leaving a surplus of $2.01. The man was in debt to the Chinese builder of his house.

4. This household includes a man, his wife, two sons, and a divorced daughter with her baby. They tapped a total of 16.3 acres of rubber land, divided into five lots. Their income for the week, earned from 146 man hours, was $160.08. In addition, one of the sons earned $440 a month as a schoolteacher and contributed most of his earnings to the household. Expenditure for the week was: $34.75 food; $9.00 on cigarettes and coffee shop; $14.00 on gasoline for the two motor scooters; $15.00 on ammunition for bird and small game hunting; and $3.00 for acid and a tin. Total expenses for the week were $75.75, leaving a balance of $84.33 excluding the schoolmaster's income. The family has no debts and they pay cash for everything they buy. The father and the schoolmaster both have a Post Office savings account, with joint deposits totaling $8,779. Earlier in the year they had spent almost $3,000 on a large addition to the house, together with other improvements. This is a quite exceptional household in many ways: all members work hard and long, and the father is anxious to take advantage of any and all modern processes that might lead to improvement in rubber trees and agriculture in general. He sent his eldest son (the schoolmaster) to the Rubber Research Institute in Kuala Lumpur for a month's course on methods of improving

rubber yields, and he was experimenting with grafting and raising hybrid seedlings to improve his trees. The father has no special experience, but is simply an unusual individual, strongly motivated to work and always ready to learn—a rural developer's dream.

5. This household comprises a man, his wife, and five of their six children. Two of the children, aged eleven and nine, assist their parents in tapping and working in the ladang or dry-rice field, but they do not earn money separately. The household owns 6.4 acres of rubber holding, but most of this is no longer productive, and the head of the household is unwilling to replant, saying he cannot afford the risk. His wife, however, is anxious to do so. Most of their income derives from tapping as coolies for a large landowner. Total earnings for the week were $19.14, of which $9.35 was spent on food and household supplies; $5.65 on cigarettes, coffee shop, betel, candy, and ice cream; 75 cents for formic acid; and $4.00 for a new water bucket with which to draw water. Total expenses were $19.75, leaving a deficit of 61 cents. The man also owed $11.00 to the village store. The wife was expert at mat making and basket weaving, but did so only to supply her own needs. The man had once specialized in making bedsteads, but had not made any for some time. He also received a "good will" pension of $8.00 a month from a former (Chinese) employer for whom he had worked for fifteen years.

6. This household consists of a man, his sister, his wife, and their two children. The three adults work as coolies for the manager of holdings belonging to an absent villager. The arrangement is that the owner gets one-third of the income, the manager one-third, and the coolies the other third. The total income for the week was $18.56. Food and household supplies cost $12.70; cigarettes, $2.80; $1.50 was spent on acid for

processing and a new knife for tapping, and one woman bought a new batik for a sarong for $5.00 Deficit for the week was $3.44.

7. This household is made up of a man, his wife, their four children, and the man's daughter by a former marriage. The man owns three acres of rubber holding, but most of the trees are old. He worked 16 hours over a three-day week and earned $10.44. His expenses were: $7.45 on food and household supplies, and $3.10 on cigarettes and coffee shop, and his wife bought two large dish covers from a traveling vendor for $1.50. Payments on a bicycle and radio were being made once a month (at $10 a month) and the man maintained that he would work a longer week when the payments were due. The deficit for the week was $1.61.

8. This household includes a man, his wife, and two of their grandsons, one of whom tapped rubber while the other was at school. The old man was too crippled to tap. The boys' father is a police detective working in Seremban, who contributes a minimum of $45 a month toward the expenses of the household and is also willing to pay various small debts incurred by his sons. The young man worked an 18-hour week on 4.2 acres of rubber and earned $13.92, of which $11 went on food and supplies. However, the two boys ate many of their meals at the coffee shop and spent $14.54 there, plus $5.00 on cigarettes and $3.80 on cards. Total expenditure for the week was $34.34. In addition, the family bought an expensive radio. The excess of expenditure over income (including the father's regular contribution) was $9.42, but this was made up by the father.

9. This household consists of a man, his wife, and five children. The eldest son, unmarried, is 24 years old and works with his father, who owns 13.1 acres of rubber land. Both are good carpenters and were sometimes employed to do house repair work in the village. During the week

they worked a total of 48 man hours in four days and earned $45.24. A total of $20.60 was spent on food and household supplies, which were supplemented from a small but well-tended vegetable garden and a daily supply of fish brought in by the father or the son, one of whom always went fishing. Five dollars was spent on cigarettes and $3.50 at the coffee shop and for ice cream. Total expenses for the week were $29.10, leaving a balance of $16.14. The household also kept a small herd of goats and about 15 head of water buffalo, both being looked after by the children.

10. A man and his son make up this household. The son works occasionally as a coolie. For the week in question he worked 15 hours on four days of the week and earned $10.44. Their house barely amounted to a roof with supports and was situated in the forecourt of the house of a kinsman with whom they ate most of their meals. The entire income was spent on cigarettes, coffee, and cards, at which the son won 65 cents.

From the above sample it would appear that the minimum household income for a week ought to be $20 if no debt is incurred. All those households with a deficit for the week earned less than $20. For some, this is a situation which they can remedy by putting in more hours, so that their deficit is somewhat the result of miscalculation. Basically, however, what is illustrated is the truism that those who are poor to begin with are likely to get poorer, and they must somehow reduce their expenditures. It is of some interest to note the possibility implied in the figures that the minimum required income applies irrespective of the size of the household; wealthier households eat more expensive food (meat, fish, poultry, and vegetables) and poorer households simply eat fewer of these as lauk or side dishes. The average sum spent on food and household supplies per person per week is $3.20, but it must be remembered that in many cases this is supplemented by fish and vegetables and occasionally by eggs produced by the household. The sum spent by adults on cigarettes and the coffee shop averages $1.61 per person per week, half the amount spent on food. There is sufficient variety of food available at a wide range of prices for a household with an income of $20 to eat fairly well and within its means. It is also noteworthy that those who own their own land with productive trees are far better off than those who have to work as coolies because they have no land or because the trees they own are no longer productive. Even though the relationship between landowner and coolie (described in detail below) is cloaked in equality, a comparison of hours worked by owners versus coolies shows that the latter put in only the barest minimum, while the former, presumably with pride of ownership, work harder. There is a wide range of incomes displayed in the sample which, although chosen at random, includes the one household in the village with an exceptionally high income. There are other households approaching the income of this exception, however, and their wealth is evident in their homes, which are more fully furnished and include many more items that are new. The poorest households have virtually no furniture except a few homemade shelves for clothes, utensils, and crockery, and the wealthiest have dining room suites (including sideboards) and living room suites with glass-fronted cupboards, armchairs, coffee tables, bookshelves, and large table radios.

The above sample was taken in a week when no religious or ritual celebrations occurred and when no household incurred any extraordinary expense. However, the religious and ritual calendars require considerable expenditures. Chief of the religious events is the Hari Raya Puasa, the month of celebration following the fasting month of Ramadan. During this month the villagers, and in fact all Malays, visit each other's homes to renew their ties, bury quarrels and in general seek the pleasure of each other's company. It is mandatory to have a large supply of cakes and sweetmeats with which to entertain the visitors, and a bewildering variety of cakes is made during the last week of Ramadan in preparation for Hari Raya. Many of the ingredients are costly (essence, eggs, flour, fruit, milk, etc.) and, in addition, every family tries to buy meat on which to feast at the end of the fast. Since each household expects visitors, the house is given a thorough cleaning, and every effort is made to have something new for the house—curtains, linoleum, furniture, and so forth. In some instances during the period of my stay, expenses for Hari Raya Puasa ran to nearly $500, which included, in two cases, a complete new suite of dining room furniture and curtains for the entire house. On the other hand, one of the poorest households rested content with a new square of linoleum on the otherwise bare floor. It was on this that visitors were invited to sit. Members of the household, especially women and children, purchase new clothes for the celebration, but here again purchases are generally within the means of the house. Other religious festivals, such as Hari Raya Haji, are not celebrated to any great extent in the village and do not involve major expenses—they are simply acknowledged.

Although Hari Raya Puasa is a predictable expenditure, it has the disadvantage of coming immediately after Ramadan, a month when work efficiency and income drop rapidly as the fast progresses. Extra work must begin at least two months before the festival, and many villagers are caught napping because they do not tap more rubber early enough. There is slight compensation in that the amount spent on food and cigarettes during the fast may be slightly less than during an ordinary month, but it is doubtful whether the savings thus effected are equal to meeting the additional expenses incurred during Hari Raya Puasa.* To meet expenses of Hari Raya Puasa and other ritual feasts (kendury), two courses are employed if the regular income is insufficient. The first is for a woman to pawn her jewelry and the second is to incur a debt with a merchant. The first course is unpopular, because it is particularly at the time of a celebration, with many visitors around, that a woman likes to show off her jewelry—and her man likes her to because it indicates how well he cares for her. A number of households go into debt at Hari Raya Puasa and when they give kendury. During the eight-month period of field work, eleven households in Jendram Hilir gave kendury. Three combined circumcision, or bersunat, with hatam koran, to mark the completion of a boy's Koranic studies. There were two weddings, three gunting rambut, or first haircut ceremonies, one funeral, one kendury to greet the return of a relative long absent from the village, and one kendury to send off a pilgrim to Mecca. The most expensive of these kendury were the two weddings, one of which cost approximately $800. and the other $500., with expenses met by both families. The cheapest ceremony was the gunting rambut, at which the meal was supplied only to near relatives living in the village, at a cost of about $35.

The income of the household is managed by the senior woman, who also spends most of it. The cash itself is usually deposited in a jar or box on a shelf in the kitchen, and the man either asks for money or helps himself, usually informing his wife. A few men keep cash from their earnings

---

*Fasting during Ramadan is confined only to the hours of daylight. At least two meals are eaten between dusk and dawn.

to pay for cigarettes and coffee. The woman buys goods from the store or sends a child and occasionally the man. In some households, money to buy clothing or to meet specific obligations is set aside in a different jar or box. Women's jewelry is kept carefully hidden—in one instance, some earrings were hidden in a chicken house, with unfortunate consequences.

Apart from those households earning less than what seems to be the necessary minimum (about $20 a week), chronic indebtedness is not a village problem, and villagers display a realistic sense of management. The correlation between income and expenditure is close, and is the result of conscious management and careful tailoring of purchases to income. In the larger expenditures on clothing, household goods, and catering, the Malay woman is a discriminating shopper who is by no means intimidated by Chinese storekeepers. The post mortem that goes on between a woman and her neighbors after she has returned from a shopping expedition—the appreciation of a good buy and of the buying skill of the shopper—is evidence of the Malay woman's concern with shopping technique and of a real understanding of the relationship between cash and goods.

What seems to be less well understood by many in the village is the sense in which money may be manipulated as noncash. Few villagers have savings accounts, and all of those who do started them when they were working outside of the village—mostly in the armed forces. The Islamic injunction against usury may in general affect the Malay attitude toward interest and investment, and it is clear from conversations with villagers that the ability of money to "work" without being considered usury is not well understood. A number of individuals defaulted on payments for articles they had purchased even though they had the money at the time, simply because they chose to undertake another obligation. For example, one man bought a radio, made a down payment, and paid two monthly installments. He then purchased a bicycle but could not afford the payments on both at the same time. He explained to me that he felt that having actually paid some cash for the radio and having the radio in hand, it was rightfully his. He would eventually pay the whole sum after he had bought his bicycle, which he needed urgently. The case seems to illustrate a widespread idea: namely that the implications of a legal contract are alien, so that the handing over of cash for an article is in itself an act of commitment. Money or cash that does not yet exist in hand is irrelevant, cash being strictly a means to an end—once the end (radio or bicycle, etc.) has been attained, the means has served its purpose.

It has been pointed out that for many households, particularly those without productive land, the amount of work put in is adjusted to the estimate of the daily needs of the household. There is little surplus income produced in the village, but what is accumulated is spent on jewelry as a form of savings (cf. Swift 1963: 136) and on house improvements. In both cases it is worth pointing out that the initiative is taken by the woman, who is also the main beneficiary. Even major expenditures such as kendury are managed by the women, who also direct or carry out the buying. Women also make a considerable contribution to earnings in the village by tapping, gardening, fishing, and making clothes, so that in any consideration of directing economic change within a village the significant role of the woman must be brought into account.

The majority of people in the village tap their own rubber trees and work for themselves. This occupation requires no form of cooperation

-92-

over and above the level of the household, and even the cooperation of members of a single household is not essential to the production of rubber. As has been mentioned, the cycle may be complete in a day, but since it is preferable to sell the keping dry it is perhaps more accurate to say that the cycle (i.e. from tapping to selling) takes a few days. Furthermore, the income is steady throughout the year, and the amount of planning and preparation required is minimal. Thus rubber economy contrasts greatly with the two major traditional occupations of village Malays—padi growing and fishing. Both of these are dependent on seasons, require extensive preparatory labor, have fluctuating yields, and have differing organizational requirements. Whereas tapping is individually based and can be carried out on a year-round basis, padi growing and, even more so, fishing are cooperatively organized and subject to seasons. For example, "the same man may be an agriculturalist at one season of the year and a fisherman at another" (Firth 1946: 23). Rice growing in particular requires considerable economic planning, because income is obtained only once or twice a year, whereas rubber yields a daily income and fishing a regular income for part of the year. As Firth has made so abundantly clear, fishing requires a complex social organization and considerable economic organization and management, leading to the dominance of interdependence among those reliant on fishing for a livelihood: One conclusion that can be drawn is that all groups in one area are closely affected by each other (cf. Firth 1946: 119). Lastly, both rice growing and fishing are accompanied by extensive ritual, which entails a number of beliefs that inform the values attached to the work of padi growing and fishing. There is no ritual associated with rubber tapping, and tapping as a human activity is evaluated as being extremely low.

Although everyone in the village is dependent on rubber tapping for their subsistence, it is significant that the term for work (kerja) is not used to describe the time and effort expended in tapping. Instead, rubber tapping is described as makan gaji, biken duit, or chari wang—all expressions meaning "to make money." The activity is also described straightforwardly as potong getah, to cut rubber. The term kerja is reserved for activities such as gardening, fishing, collecting firewood, working in the ladang on padi bukit (dry rice), or in the sawah (wet-rice field), and sometimes for food preparation, cooking, and clothes washing. That is to say, all activities that contribute directly and in kind to the subsistence of the household are thought of as being work, but not those activities, such as rubber tapping, which contribute only indirectly. This classification of types of effort is indicative of the "moral" attitude of village Malays to priorities with respect to economic activities. Those tasks classified as kerja are thought of as tasks for which the labor expended is worthwhile, and to do such work contributes to one's dignity. These tasks are inherently part of Malay adat, which, together with Islam, is the touchstone of worthiness. Furthermore, these are tasks that can be conducted only by orangorang kampong, as opposed to orangorang bandar, whose only concern is money. Rubber tapping is inseparable from money, and making money is the only raison d'etre for tapping. There is no dignity attached to rubber tapping or makan gaji, even though they may be highly necessary, and any task or activity is likely to take precedence in the village evaluation of worthiness. Even though village Malays, such as those of Jendram, are totally dependent on the income from rubber, there is no moral incentive that would lead them to adopt a progressive attitude, as expressed through caring for their holdings or learning modern techniques

-94-

of grafting, tapping, and so forth. It may also be worthwhile to suggest that this "value" judgment has some effect on the performance of Malays in urban settings, where they are employed in factories and offices.

The majority of Malays employed in unskilled jobs in Kuala Lumpur, Petaling Jaya, and other urban centers have come from villages on the west coast and have had no more than primary schooling. There is no reason to think that their values with respect to work priorities and worthiness are very different from those held in the village. The work they do in the city is not kerja, but makan gaji. The sense of obligation and honor in performing work does not carry over to makan gaji, though some changes in this attitude have probably taken place. This, and another factor mentioned below, may also help to explain the one favorable estimation of Malay performance that I obtained from a non-Malay employer, in this case the manager of the RIDA boatyard in Kuala Trengganu. There the Malays were successfully carrying out their traditional task of boat building, a task which is subsidiary to the fishing that provides the direct subsistence, but which is ritually and socially part and parcel of the entire fishing complex.

Of equal possible significance in attempting to gauge the values of villagers with respect to work is the complex of implications of the term and institution of tolong menolong. This term describes the social aspect of the relationship between one who works for another, while the term bagi dua describes the economic aspect. Tolong menolong means, more or less, reciprocal help, and bagi dua means "to go halves," referring to the fact that the owner and the coolie each receive half the proceeds from the sale of rubber.

The number of households employing coolies varies, but at the time

-95-

of field work it was ten, and the number of coolies working was fifty-two. The employing households own an average of thirteen acres of smallholding, and in seven of these the individual male owner is elderly and no longer able or willing to do much tapping, although he may personally sell the rubber. The use of the term tolong menolong to describe a relationship between a coolie and a landowner indicates that though there may indeed be an economic discrepancy between the two, their social status is nominally equal. The mutual agreement to employ and to work is an agreement between equals, a factor also indicated in the sharing of the proceeds. The term tolong menolong is most commonly employed within the domestic context, as when members of a family give each other a hand in preparing for a kendury and expect the same service to be performed when it comes their turn to hold a kendury. The idea of doing each other favors and of helping each other in times of need (tolong menolong) is an integral part of the meaning of kinship and friendship between people, and is at the same time a sign of respect and equality. When applied to coolies, it implies that the relationship is first and foremost a personal one, analogous to a kinship relation in which each partner is rendering the other a needed service. In many cases, the coolies are kin to the landowner, and in other cases, the term saudara is used of such relations, even though they may not be actual kin. The relationship is clearly lopsided, and strains do arise. Owners continually complain to others about their coolies and indicate how much more rubber would be obtained if they were doing it themselves. One old man confided to me how dissatisfied he was with two of his grandsons who worked for him and who produced not more than three keping a day. Consequently, they were always coming to him for an advance or a loan, which, he said, would not be repaid. The status of the coolie is often explained by stating how the man is in fact doing the landowner a service in providing him with labor, because otherwise he would not be able to get a fraction of the rubber he now taps. Occasionally the reference is made to the Islamic ideal of charity as a motive on the part of wealthier landowners employing coolies. In many cases, the situation is mutually beneficial and advantageous, but in some cases it is clear that the employer has one or two coolies more than he really needs.

Employment within the village is not thought of as an impersonal relationship bound by a legal contract or subject to sanctions outside of the persons involved in the relationship. It is a social relationship first and foremost, and it is this view of employment that is carried from the village to the towns. No doubt it becomes modified there, but the moral aspect, in which both partners are of equal status, may still remain. The obligation to observe the contract as first priority, especially a contract in which makan gaji rather than kerja is concerned, is unlikely to rank high in the Malay scale of values. A visit to a sick kinsman, a religious observance, or even the forwarding of a personal relationship by a visit and conversation is likely to count for more than getting a job done. Something akin to this scale of values was implicit in the thinking and attitudes of those Malays with whom I talked who lived in Kuala Lumpur but who were originally from Jendram Hilir and neighboring villages. One young man had recently been upset because he was spoken to harshly by his foreman and threatened with dismissal. It seemed that he had gone off to Ipoh for four days on hearing that his uncle was sick and expected to die. He had not informed his foreman or the floor manager, and, in fact, he did not seem to recognize that he was expected to do so. For most Malays, fulfillment of kin obligations takes first place in relation to fulfillment of the conditions of an impersonal contract, such as that existing between employer and employee (an attitude furthered by the often impersonal nature of the place of work and the relations between management and employee). The village model of employment as a reciprocal relation between equals doing each other a service and conducted personally is often carried from the village to the town.

The above account of rubber tapping and organization of work in Jendram Hilir should be compared with that given by Swift for a village in Jelebu. By and large the process is similar, so I will here note some of the differences. The term tolong menolong is not mentioned as being applied to the relationship between landowners and coolies, although Swift does note that the upper hand in the relationship is held by the coolie, who can, and does, withdraw his labor and demand loans which he does not always repay. This derives from the fact that at the time of Swift's field work, there was a labor shortage. The author notes (Swift 1965: 61-62) that: "durable owner-tapper relations are all between relatives or affines . . . . the tapper is able to regard the holding as to some extent his, and the owner to regard giving employment to a relative as a worthy act." This is equally applicable to Jendram Hilir. Swift notes that: "competition of other forms of work may attract a man from rubber tapping." As noted above, this may well be because rubber tapping is at the bottom of the villagers' scale of values concerning working activities, and it takes very little competition to draw a man away from tapping. One slight difference is the ratio of division of proceeds: in Jelebu the division is six parts to the owner and four to the tapper as compared to the equal sharing in Jendram (bagi dua).*

Although rubber tapping is far and away the most important productive activity undertaken by the villagers of Jendram Hilir, there are
a number of other activities which contribute to the economics of various
households. Twenty households between them cultivate a total of 48.5
acres of ladang or padi bukit, i.e. dry rice, and on the same land a few
vegetables are also grown. Some of these acres are given over to sawah
or wet-rice cultivation, using water from nearby streams led off by man-
made channels. At the time of field work there were a few acres of un-
cultivated rice land. The households that own rice land tend to be related, and the land, most of which is located in two main spots near the
village, is cleared simultaneously by each household, though there is
little or no cooperation between households. The holding of each household is clearly marked by either a bund or a path and is denoted by the
presence of a pondok or shelter in the field. Work in the field is entirely
a household affair, with women and children giving more of their time
than the men. All members cooperate in clearing the land, which is
sometimes burned first, and in planting the seed. While the grain is rip-
ening, women and children spend all day in the pondok scaring away
birds and vermin. They cook their meals there and sometimes sleep there
at night. Tin cans hung on lines are strung out across the field from the
pondok, and when the lines are jogged the cans rattle and scare the birds.
Everyone helps in the harvest, with the adults doing most of the cutting,

---

*The traditional Malaysian institution of reciprocal help, best known
by the Javanese term gotong royong, is familiar in Jendram and is more
usually called kerja bersamasama (to work together). Villagers all agree
that this is something from the past and no longer a part of adat.

using the traditional tuai blade which cuts one stem at a time, and the
children and women doing most of the winnowing and packing of the
grain into the sacks. Unless a man needs money for the day or feels like
going to the coffee shop, he prefers to work in the rice field, especially
during harvest time (about February). At that time, the whole family
more or less lives in the pondok, enjoying the picnic atmosphere and ex-
changing visits with kin in neighboring fields. No help outside the household is employed in the rice field, and the produce is used by the household. The local rice, described as wangi (fragrant) is much preferred to
store-bought rice. Especially prized by those who grow it is the pulut, or
glutinous rice, used principally in making sweet cakes. Some of the rice
may be given as a gift to a kinsman, and some is always reserved for use
in kendury.

Other crops are planted somewhat haphazardly in the dry-rice fields
and include corn, melons, eggplant, and squash. For the most part, these
are consumed by the household, if not by vermin, but occasionally one
or two men produce a small surplus which is sold through the village store.

One man in the village, whose rubber trees have more or less ceased
production, has taken advantage of the government's offer of new seedlings
and a loan enabling him to replant. To tide himself and his family over
the interim of seven years before the newly planted trees begin to yield,
he has cleared about four acres of land and started a market garden, growing principally chili peppers, pineapples, eggplant, and bananas. These
he sells four times a week to a Chinese stallholder in the market at Kajang.
His income varies from about $20 a week to $35, but he spoke highly of
the pleasure he derived from the cultivation of the plants, and he thought
he would carry on even when his rubber trees began to yield.

In addition to those who grow vegetables in the ladang, 47 households in the village have small kitchen gardens (kebon). These are cultivated exclusively by women and children, and the main crops are chili
peppers, manioc, eggplant, leaf greens, pineapples, and bananas. A
few tomatoes and beans are grown. Although these gardens are not tended
every day, they receive regular care throughout the year. Most are not
well kept, especially if compared with Chinese vegetable gardens. A
further source of food and income is the dusun (orchard) and the fruit trees
grown around the house. Dusun really describes fruit trees growing away
from the house, for in Jendram Hilir there are no planned orchards. Chief
of the trees are: durian, mango, mangosteen, langsat, rambutan, coconut palm, areca nut, and the sireh leaf bush (the latter two are used in
the preparation of the betel quid). Some houses have a few coffee bushes,
but no intensive effort is made to grow coffee. Of all the tree crops, the
durian is the most highly prized and is the only one that receives any special attention. When the durian ripen, many households build a small
pondok (shelter), where a member sleeps during the night so that he or
she will be on hand to pick up the fruit when they fall. Of fruits, too, the
durian is the most highly prized, both by the villagers and by the Chinese.
Although coconut is an essential ingredient in Malay cooking, no household in the village has enough palms to meet its own needs, and most of
the coconut used is bought from the store, which receives its supply from
a Chinese dealer.

The village is situated close by three rivers and a number of small
streams and ponds, all of which are well supplied with fish. Six men in
the village own canoes and use them regularly for fishing trips on the
largest river, the Sungei Langat. Most of the catch is eaten by the

household, but occasionally, if the woman does not feel like drying the surplus fish, they are sold to a neighbor or through the village store. None of the fishermen has ever considered fishing for a living, and all consider it a sport and a pleasurable pastime. The women and children of most village households regularly fish in the streams, ponds, and ditches using rod and line and traps. Occasionally the boys use nets. For many villagers, fish is the chief source of protein, and it is a major food source for households with little income. The usual pattern is for a woman, usually an older woman no longer able or willing to tap rubber, to go with a child to one of the streams or to a favorite spot after morning coffee and to return at about midday. Where there is no older woman, other members of the household, who may have been tapping during the day, go fishing for an hour or two in the late afternoon.

A regularly recurring activity of considerable economic importance to all households is the cutting and collection of firewood. The largest source of supply is dead rubber trees and trees from the secondary jungle surrounding the village. Firewood collection is carried out at least once a week by most households and is performed mainly by women with the assistance of children. The wood is used for cooking. Other occasional collecting includes sago leaf for thatching (from the palms growing wild in the swampy land north of the village) and rattan for weaving baskets and mats. The thatch is made by one or two men in the village, for their own use or at special request, and is used to repair roofing. If a whole new roof is required, the batons are bought from a thatchmaker in Jendram Ulu or, more often, from a Chinese thatchmaker in Dengkil. The leaves are sewn onto a baton about four feet long, and each baton sells for seven cents (poor quality) or 25 cents good quality (generally using nipa palm

leaf). Although about half the houses in the village are thatched, zinc
roofing is now becoming the standard.

Almost all the men of the village are, to varying degrees, able
carpenters, and a few are sufficiently skillful to be able to build a house
and make furniture. None do so for a living, however, or rely on their
skill for any part of their income. Forty-three structures in the village
were built by villagers, the rest being built by Chinese contractors.

The village therefore has no economic specialization apart from
such roles as schoolmaster, imam, and storekeeper, and there is little
or no economic interdependence within the village. Each household is a
separate economic unit, producing its own rubber or providing labor and
dependent for every other aspect of its economic survival on the Chinese
merchants. The ancillary activities mentioned above afford only a small
contribution to the economic survival of the household. Although the village is not bound together as a cooperating economic unit, the pattern of
work organization imposed by rubber tapping gives the daily life of each
household a uniform appearance and, with certain notable exceptions,
the approximate parity of income again provides for little variation between households.

Though rubber tapping is the major economic activity, it is held in
low esteem. As already noted, it does not have the dignity of kerja, and
it is described as kotor (dirty) and lifeless (tidak ada semangat) in contrast
to activities such as padi growing and fishing. For many households, only
a minimum amount of time is spent tapping, which leaves plenty of time
for doing other things. Many of the young unmarried men of the village
either do not tap at all or tap very irregularly and specifically in order to
earn cigarette money. Most of their morning is spent leafing through old

newspapers, talking, listening to the radio, and drinking coffee. The afternoon is often spent sleeping or playing "twenty-one," and the evening goes like the morning. All of these young men spoke of their desire for money and of the lack of opportunity to earn any other than by going to work in Kuala Lumpur. The chance of service in the armed forces is the brightest prospect for them to accumulate money, a factor also noted by Swift for Jelebu. Most of the young men (the geng) participated with great enthusiasm in the weekly drill conducted by a regular army NCO on the school football field.

For the other male age groups of the community, leisure time is passed with conversation. After a cleanup following the completion of the day's tapping many men go to the coffee shop for an hour or so and then take an afternoon nap. They may spend some time playing with the children before the evening meal, and after the meal they go back to the coffee shop for a drink and a chat till about 10:30 P.M. Bird and small game hunting and fishing have already been mentioned as pastimes for some men.

The women of the village never visit the coffee shop. Their intra-village outings are confined to shopping at the store (a chore they share with the children), and visiting—usually confined within the loosely defined clusters of houses. Domestic tasks such as looking after children, preparing and cooking meals, and cleaning the house occur at more or less the same time on each day of the week. When the regular tasks are in abeyance, such tasks as sewing and clothes mending demand attention. The only domestic task that takes a woman out of the house is clothes washing, which is done by most women each day, early in the morning. A number of houses have their own wells, but many share one, and for

-104-

those women who share a well, clothes washing provides an enjoyable opportunity for gossip. In the organization and conduct of the daily household tasks, there is little distinction between married and unmarried women, young or old. Depending on the exact composition of a household, various tasks such as fishing, clothes washing, cooking, looking after children, and so on are divided among the women, with the senior women exercising some prerogative of choice. There is, however, some distinction of status among women in the village, and it is most clearly reflected in the freedom of movement and relative relaxing of certain standards of modesty as a woman achieves middle age and the status of grandmother or mother beyond childbearing.

When a girl approaches puberty, she dresses more or less exclusively in the traditional sarong, whereas previously she had worn shorter, Western-style dresses as well as the sarong. From this time on until marriage, her movements are restricted, and any journey, particularly by public transport, is undertaken only with a chaperone (traveling to school is excepted). When a woman reaches the age of about forty, or when she has finished child bearing, she no longer wears her hair loose or has it styled, but wears only the traditional bun style. Whereas until this stage women are extremely careful to be properly dressed at all times, even within the house, women who achieve the third stage may often be seen by the public, though within the confines of their own homes, in a state of partial undress. They are also free to travel alone and undertake the extensive program of jalanjalan or social visiting described above. Women of this age speak freely in the company of their menfolk, often smoke cigarettes in public, and invariably chew betel. Furthermore, women of this status (for which there appears to be no name) are influential in all decision-making, both within the household—especially with regards to economics—and, indirectly, in the village. It is these women who largely determine the household budget, who do the major shopping, and who spend most of a household's income.

In any attempt to assess the values that underlie economic activity and behavior in a Malay village, some consideration must be given to the notion of rezeki, or economic destiny, a concept described by Swift (1965: 29-30). Rezeki is the idea that one's economic success or failure is only in part one's own responsibility and that for the most part what is to be achieved will come about only through the will of God. As noted by Swift, it is invoked mostly in exoneration of failure and as an excuse to give up after a setback. For the villagers of Jendram Hilir, the concept does not seem to provide a major principle in their economic thinking or conduct, and is instead confined to the realm of the abstract. Thus the failure of man to make a go of a taxi business and the failure of a cooperative were attributed to: (1) the inability of Malays to compete with Chinese, especially in view of the latter's evil practices (the Chinese mechanic was said to have sabotaged the Malay taxi) and (2) the incompetence of the official who set up the cooperative and who, it was said, absconded with the funds. Only in a general way was the idea of rezeki invoked, when it was observed with a sigh and a laugh that Malays are village people (orangorang kampong) and cannot be expected to manage such things. If it is anyone's responsibility, it is that of the government, who should lead the orangorang kampong to economic prosperity.

Of at least equal importance in the formulation of village attitudes toward economic matters is the idea that work relationships are social relationships and, as such, are subject to the same canons and tenets that

govern and control the smooth functioning of those social relationships.
The blueprint for social relationships is the pattern of expectations and
conduct pertinent to keluarga and saudara—equality and mutual respect,
a perfect gearing together of people involved personally with each other.
Although not evident in a rubber-tapping village, the ideal of interdependence is basic to the social organization of both padi growing and fishing. Insofar as the village Malay is involved in an activity being conducted by many persons, then the success of performance depends first on
the way in which the individuals can accommodate each other personally
in terms of temperament and mutual consideration and then on how clearly defined the work role is and how clearly marked or obvious the interdependence. The description of employer-coolie relations as tolong
menolong is indicative of the ideal expressed above, and Firth, in his
analysis of Kelantan fishing crews, constantly stresses the mutual adjust-
ment of members of a crew. "The mutual relations between an expert
and his crew are governed not by any set formula of rights and duties, but
by a number of practical assumptions about what is reasonable in the circumstances of their work" (Firth 1946: 104). It may be the approximate
conformity to these norms that has led to the success of Malay performance
in the RIDA boatyards in Kuala Trengganu, where work teams, each organized by rank and each rank with an assigned task, are set to the building of a boat. The clear formulation of status and the clear indication
of interdependence may also partially explain why village Malays are at-
tracted to the police and the army, though there are doubtless many more
factors (the traditional hierarchical status structure of Malay society may
be one such factor).

　　With respect to rubber tapping as opposed to other rural Malay activities, it is not an "institutionalized" activity and it has no place in Malay adat. It has no traditions and no ritual. It provides no food, it has no life, and it has no traditionally sanctioned pattern of conduct or organization. It merely provides cash and ties the Malay permanently to the Chinese. The pattern of rubber tapping is in direct contrast to the pattern discerned as typical of the east coast, where economic activities are incorporated into wide-ranging institutional networks which make up a coherent cultural pattern. This in turn "contains values—e.g., social and economic ones, which are formed and established in the course of generations" (Tjoa 1963: 253). The basic economic activity, rubber tapping, has no part in the tradition and adat of village Malays and is not integrated into any other aspect of culture. It is, therefore, not surprising that Malay culture in Jendram seems to be falling apart rather than sticking together. A number of values and attitudes with respect to work and economic relationships can be discerned in the village deriving from the status of rubber tapping and from the basically domestic orientation of Malay social relations. It is the principles of this village value system that are carried into towns and, it is suggested, color the performance of Malays working in the urban setting.

The sociological basis of this value system is the subject of the next chapter.

CHAPTER 4

In his study of the indigenous political systems of Selangor, Perak,
and Negri Sembilan just prior to the establishment of British control in
1874, Gullick notes that in the former states: "the lack of any predomi-
nant social system precluded the possibility of a political system based on
a social system" (Gullick 1958: 37). The basic unit on which the political
system was built was the village, whose population: "had no basis of association in groups larger than villages. In terms of descent, kinship and
culture [villages] were so heterogeneous and discrete as to have no natural alignment into larger groups" (Gullick 1958: 43). Villages were sited
along the river banks, but settlement was transitory and impermanent, deriving in large part from the unstable political conditions of the times
(Gullick 1958: 43). A village had its headman, who may or may not have
been a member of the aristocracy, and the major part of the population
comprised the subject class (rayat). "The original focus of each village
settlement had been a founding family led by a headman . . . . The
founder and first headman brought with him some of his kindred, by blood
and affinity . . . but the strongest tie of all was common cultural origin"
(Gullick 1958: 32). Income was partially derived from the sale of forest

products and of small crop surpluses, such as padi and spices, and from occasional odd jobs such as boat poling. The political unity of the village
was tenuous and the authority of the headman is described by Gullick as
being very limited (1958: 31).

The village of Jendram Hilir provides a specific example conform-
ing to the above general pattern. The founding ancestors were two brothers married to two sisters who emigrated from Sumatra in the later 1870s.
The reason for their emigration as given by their descendants was their desire to avoid the harshness of Dutch rule. With them they brought their
children and some friends and founded a village some thirteen miles
northeast of the present village on the banks of the Sungei Langat. In the
mid 1880s, or perhaps as late as 1890, the founders, their friends, and
fellow villagers moved to the site of the present village. The reason for
the move is uncertain, but it is said to be because of a desire for more
land, which was available at Jendram. In the first decade of the twentieth century, the villagers began to plant rubber, and their plantings increased in the second decade. Between 1915 and 1920 a new section of
the village was formed by the settlement of a couple of Mandiling families from Sumatra who, it is claimed, may use the title of "Raja." From
the time of their settlement, there has been friction between the original
settlers and the Mandiling. The original settlers regard themselves as
members of two interrelated keterunan (translated literally as generations
and approximately as lineages) named Ramba and Kepunohan, terms that
are said to denote the region of origin of each (i.e. the two brothers and
the two sisters). Ramba and Kepunohan comprise an alliance faction in
opposition to the Mandiling, but this factionalism is relevant to village
life in a minor way only and is not even sufficiently strong for it to be

-110-

claimed that such opposition creates a village unit.

Jendram Hilir is one village in a larger mukim under the administrative responsibility of a penghulu, a professional civil servant appointed
by the state government and resident in Dengkil. At the time of field
work, Jendram Hilir had no headman (ketua kampong), as the former incumbent had retired. The acting ketua kampong, a Mandiling and secretary of the local UMNO cell, had been nominated by the penghulu. The
mukim is incorporated into the district (daerah) of Ulu Langat under the
administrative control of the district officer, whose headquarters are in
Kajang. This political hierarchy, which of course extends upward to the
state and the Federation, claims no loyalty from the villager, who is involved only in the most formal way possible. In other words, there has
been no change in the relationship of the village to the state, there being
no association between the social system and the political system. Little
or no political action is initiated from the village, and village involvement is almost entirely a result of action from above. Political officials
above the village level are professional civil servants and seldom native
to the areas they administer, which thereby increases the separation between village and state. At the individual level, the relationship between
officials and villagers is a formal and impersonal one, hence undesirable
to the village Malay. The "Westernization" of these officials, together
with their educational level, also separate them from the sympathies of
the village. On the other hand, there is an undoubted emotional integration of the village with higher levels of authority, although these levels
are relatively ineffective and are important only symbolically. The loyalty of villagers to the Sultan and their respect for the Mentri Besar (Prime
Minister) of the state is marked. If a state official has a title and can therefc

be assigned a place in the traditional status hierarchy, he is closely linked with the villagers. The wealth and pomp of the sultanate are topics of conversation and subject for pride among many in the village, and the Sultan is viewed as a representative of Malay power, culture, and wealth in opposition to the Chinese. Closely tied to this view is the high regard with which the Yang di-Pertuan Agong (Supreme Head) is held as a symbol of the primacy of Malays in the land.

This incorporation of the Malay villager into an expanding political hierarchy, albeit only at a ceremonial and ritual level, is periodically activated by the appearance of the Sultan, a prince, or the Mentri Besar in villages and mukim for the purpose of opening schools, mosques, or other public buildings or performing other ceremonial duties. The contrast between these dignitaries and the "strictly business" image of the district officer and politicians in general is marked.

Religious organization provides another semi-political structure into which the village and villagers can consider themselves to be actively incorporated at a higher level, and with which they are in sympathy. The grouping of mukim into waliah or religious districts is brought to life during the time of fasting, in the organization of Koran readings, and in the discussion of religious affairs within the village when any decisions must be transmitted into the larger structure.

Although the village has a tenuous social structure, it cannot be described as a social unit. It is simply that the village is, by and large, a bounded unit of residence within which the activities and interpersonal relationships of individual Malays are acted out. That this is so is the principal justification for taking the village as a unit of research and description.

Most characteristically, a Malay village comprises a number of houses strung out along both sides of a road or path. A village can be several miles from one end to the other—Jendram Hilir stretches for two and a half miles, with one satellite inland kampong that has become virtually an independent village (and therefore not included in the present study) and another small kampong also located inland off the road. There are, of course, variations, one of the chief being that of a village comprised of a number of hamlets scattered among rice fields, a pattern found in Jendram Ulu and described by Jay (1964) for Perak and Dobby (1957) for rice-growing regions. Another variation found within the mukim is the nucleated village (such as Sungei Marab and Sungei Buah), but by and large the ribbon pattern is the most typical. Such a pattern makes difficult, if not impossible, any day-to-day contact between members of households living at different ends of the village or at various points distant from each other. Social coherence is not a primary consideration of Malays when setting up a village, and any unity that comes about must be the result either of imposition or major effort and not the result of the ties between individuals that make for constant overlap of their individual interests.

Ease of communication with the outside world seems to be an overriding consideration or function of Malay village siting. Jendram Hilir is on a secondary asphalted road and is serviced by a Chinese-owned bus line operating between Kajang, Bangi, and Dengkil. The bus runs regularly on the hour between the hours of 6 A.M. to 7 P.M. Connection can be made in Kajang to all parts of Malaya (either direct or viâ Kuala Lumpur). A number of dirt roads and paths connect the various Malay kampong in the area, and it can reasonably be claimed that travel in and out of the kampong at all times of the year is very easy (although it is somewhat more difficult from kampong in the interior). Chinese dealers and whole-salers supply the village store with fresh and manufactured products, and an Indian bakery in Kuala Lumpur delivers wrapped bread three times a week. There is no postal service, but there is a postal agent (wakil pos) in Jendram Ulu who receives mail for the village and sends it around with the bus driver.

Seventy-four households in the village own at least one bicycle, and all the others usually have access to one. Of the five men who own motor scooters, three travel daily to jobs outside the village (two watchmen and one schoolteacher). There is one car in the village, a 1947 Austin, which occasionally putters as far as the Chinese mechanic and once, during my stay, was able to carry a load of rubber, though it had to be pushed the last two miles. Another car is owned by the headmaster of the school, a recent arrival in the village. On weekends and holidays many cars can be seen in the village belonging to relatives from Kuala Lumpur and other towns, and these relatives often take their village kinsmen for Sunday after-noon drives through the countryside or sometimes as far as the beach at Morib, about forty miles distant.

Most of the village houses stand in cleared yards, surrounded on the outer fringes by fruit trees, such as durian, mango, mangosteen, coconut, and rambutan, and by flowers, principally hibiscus and orchid. The houses themselves are of wood and are of one basic design with many variations: thus there are "L"-shaped, "I"-shaped and "T"-shaped houses, houses with kitchens at ground level and with raised kitchens, one-room houses and multi-roomed houses. All are raised off the ground on piles from two to six feet high. The space underneath is used for odd jobs, food preparation, children's games, and storage. One can see piles of firewood, rubber, fishing traps and baskets, nets, mortars and pestles, and junk. Roofs are either of nipa thatch or zinc, and some have both, since the thatch helps to keep the house cooler. Most houses in the village are in a good state of repair and all are graced by banked wooden ledges on which potted flowers are kept. Other, smaller structures dot the yards, including chicken houses, wood sheds, tempat getah, outhouses, wells, and pondok, i. e. shelters for various and sundry purposes. Some houses have a corral or pen for the kerbau or water buffalo. Nonresidential dwellings in the village include a mosque that was recently built by the state to a design chosen by the village mosque committee. The mosque in a Malay village is often the social center of the village where the menfolk congregate in the evening to talk after prayers. The mosque in Jendram Hilir is rarely used as a social gathering place, however. Male conviviality focuses on the coffee shops. The mosque is situated about midway in the village, next to the school (sekolah kebangsaan) and the schoolmaster's house. About three-quarters of a mile from the mosque is a surau, or prayer house, a primitive structure in which men who live too far from the mosque may gather to pray. The balai rayat, or "people's hall," is a concrete structure where village meetings, adult education classes, or any other official or semiofficial meetings are called. It is painted blue and white and hung with posters, and it is furnished with some desks, cupboards, tables, and chairs. The Women's Institute meets in a special hut, half-timber, half-chicken wire, located toward one end of the village. Two general stores, a rubber-buying store, two coffee shops, and two houses with additional rooms built on to be used as stores complete the inventory of nonresidential buildings in Jendram.

Houses tend to cluster together, each cluster being separated by trees and bushes or even fences. Rubber holdings often border the road, separating houses from each other, and the entire village is surrounded by rubber smallholdings (see map). There are a few fruit trees planted together away from houses which might qualify as dusun (orchards), and there are some small sawah (wet-rice) fields bordering the road and ladang (dry-rice) fields inland. In front of some houses, bordering the road, are small pondok which are used variously as bus stops, places for selling fruit to passing motorists, and places to sit and talk.

The house is probably the most highly valued material possession of the village Malay. Not only does it frequently represent his greatest single investment of wealth but it is also the center and focus of all that is vital in his emotional, social, and cultural life. Only in one sphere, the religious, is the mosque more of a focus than the home, but then only to the male and not the female, who worships in the house. The meaning of house and household to a Malay villager is somewhat analogous to that implied for the Englishman in the saying that an "Englishman's home is his castle." The house represents and encompasses values, emotions, ambitions, motivations, and sentiments (cf. Djamour 1959: 39, 52).

The majority of houses in the village have at least three rooms, including a reception room in the front of the house, a bedroom, and a kitchen. Most houses have more than one bedroom, and many also have what amounts to an entrance hall and a number of alcoves. The reception room is the most elaborately furnished, usually with a suite of rattan or cane furniture and a glass-fronted cupboard for glassware, trinkets, trophies, ceremonial betel sets, and various odds and ends. Plastic flowers, colored portraits of the King, Queen, Sultan, Sultana, and occasionally the Prime Minister, along with a large number of family photographs and commercial posters and calendars decorate the walls. Windows are curtained and there is usually a framed quotation from the Koran above the door. Bedrooms too are often fully furnished, especially the main bedroom which usually has a large double bed covered with an elaborate spread, a wardrobe, and open shelves for clothes and towels. All visitors are welcomed in the front room, and the men are entertained there while the women repair to a back room or to the kitchen. The kitchen is the chief room of the house for all but formal occasions. Most members of the household spend most of their time there and usually eat together there. The kitchen contains a raised hearth, and cooking is done mainly with wood, with the smoke escaping through the roof. All around hang pots, pans, and various utensils, including a large variety of cake molds. Bottles and tins used for storage are kept either on open shelves or in a wire-fronted cupboard together with saucers and plates. Cups may either be stacked on the shelves or hung from hooks. Other essential utensils found in all households are a small mortar and pestle for crushing peppers and spices, a stone slab and rolling pin, a coconut grater, and assorted knives and spoons. All households except the poorest keep a large supply of crockery with which to entertain visitors. A visitor will always be offered coffee and cake, and most visitors from outside the village stay for a meal. When there are visitors, the men eat in the front room, separately from the women, using a special mat (tipar) and eating with their fingers. When a family dines alone, men and women generally eat together in the kitchen. Three meals a day are usual. Breakfast includes coffee and, optionally, cakes, leftover curry and rice, and sometimes bread. The midday meal always includes freshly-cooked rice and a number of lauk, or side dishes, one or more of which is cooked with chili pepper.

If the side dish is not spiced, then a <u>sambal</u> or chili relish is served. The most popular <u>sambal</u> is made with either shrimp paste (<u>belachan</u>) or a small dried fish of piquant flavor (<u>ikan bilis</u>). The chili provides the <u>pedas</u>, or heat, that is an absolutely essential part of Malay taste. The evening meal may sometimes be specially cooked or may comprise the leftovers from midday. The common drinks, all served very sweet, are coffee, tea, Ovaltine, milo, water, and lemonade (preferably red). When visitors are present, cigarettes are placed on the mat for all to help themselves after the meal.[*] Finger bowls are always supplied. Just as the house is the set-ting for all that is most important in Malay social life, the meal is the event at which human relations are nurtured and proclaimed.

As mentioned above, the house, and particularly the reception room (though sometimes a bedroom or alcove), is a place of worship for both men and women—exclusively so for women. At least twice a day, but often five times a day, at least one of the women of the house changes her clothes and prays. If he is in the house at the time for prayer, a man will also pray.

Since the major social activities and relationships of the Malay vil-lager receive expression within the house, it follows that the house and the household are the only meaningful social units in Malay life. The house-hold is a group of people mutually and intimately dependent on each other for fulfillment and support. A household is a commensal group which also

---

[*]Cigarettes have completely superseded betel as a sign of hospital-ity, but older women and some older men still chew betel, using old tins and boxes for storage. The special betel sets (<u>tempat sireh</u>) are kept for show and brought out only on ceremonial occasions, when they are not necessarily used. Cigars and pipes are also smoked by men, and some women chew tobacco.

sleeps together, works together, and budgets in common. It is a group of people related together through primary kinship and affinal ties, i.e. ties which carry with them the maximum expectations of emotional support and legal rights and duties.

The kinship composition of households is shown in Table 4.

Table 4

Kinship Composition of Households

Relationship pattern	Number of households	Number of individuals
A. Headed by parent(s)		
1. Husband, Wife, Children	38 (35%)	183 (32%)
2. Husband, Wife	7	14
3. Single (widow/er, divorced, bachelor, spinster)	7	7
4. One parent, Children	5	17
5. Parents, Children, Adopted children	11	60
Total	68 (65%)	281 (50%)
B. Headed by grandparent(s) or great-grandparent(s)		
1. Great-grandparents, Children (+ spouse), Grandchildren (+ spouse), Great-grandchildren	2	24
2. Grandparent(s), Children (+ spouse), Grandchildren	15	120
3. Grandparent(s), Grandchildren	4	19
Total	21 (19%)	163 (30%)

Table 4 (continued)

Relationship pattern	Number of households	Number of individuals
C. Headed by siblings		
1. Sisters (widow), Children (+ spouse), Grandchildren	1	10
2. Brothers (+ spouse), Children (+ spouse), Grandchildren	1	10
3. Brothers (+ spouse), Children	2	14
4. Brother/sister (+ spouse), Children	2	15
5. Brother/sister (divorced), Children	1	4
6. Brothers	1	2
Total	8 (7%)	55 (10%)
D. Polygynous	2	19
E. One common parent or grandparent		
1. Husband, Wife, Son, Grandson, Grandchildren	1	6
2. Husband, Wife, Child, Grandchildren, Sibling's child	1	7
3. Husband, Wife, Children, Children	1	8
4. Husband, Wife, Children, Son's wife's children	1	8

Table 4 (continued)

Relationship pattern		Number of households		Number of individuals	
5. Husband, Wife, Adopted grand-children		1		4	
6. Mother, Female friend, Children		1		4	
	Total	6	(5%)	37	(6%)
F. Non-Malay		3	(4%)	16	(4%)
	TOTAL	108		571	

Sixty-five per cent of the households in the village are, basically, made up of an elementary family, and 20 per cent comprise families that are continuous, i. e. families that include three or four generations. If category "C" is added, 26 per cent of all households are made up of versions of the extended family—vertical and/or lateral. The remainder are miscellaneous. With the exception of the polygynous households, they are the result of incidental circumstances in the lives of individuals sufficiently irregular as not to form a pattern over time. Eleven households in "A" have adopted children, and in one "E" household the grandparents adopted the grandchildren because the parents were dead. The over-all pattern of household composition, showing a dominance of the nuclear family which features the marital couple, is in keeping with the bilateral nature of Malay kinship and the individual focus of Malay social relationships. The pattern of household composition is quite comparable to that described by Djamour (1959: 53-60) for Singapore Malays.

Many of the village households are informally grouped together to form clusters of neighbors. In most cases, these clusters are of houses actually contiguous to each other, but in one or two cases the clusters can only be described as social, since the houses are widely separated. A contiguous house cluster is sometimes marked off by a fence of bushes, or even a specially erected fence on each side (the road and the rubber holding at front and back provide natural boundaries). There is no name for these clusters,* and they do not seem to conform exactly to the sort of cluster denoted by the term kampong, which implies the unity of a compound. There are eleven reasonably well-distinguished clusters in the village, ranging in size from three to nine households. There are also a number of households which are not incorporated into a cluster. There is nothing formal in the social significance of these clusters. They cannot be described as any part of the social structure of the village, though they do provide a vague setting for more intensely concentrated social interaction. A cluster is basically a group of neighboring households whose members, by virtue of their proximity in space and kinship, have most to do with each other during the course of the day. The origin of these clusters is primarily from inheritance and coresidence of siblings and/or parent and child. In some cases, the houses are some distance apart, but the household members interact with great frequency; whereas in two other cases, households located physically within a cluster have little to do with members of the cluster and so are not really part of the social aggregate. These latter examples stem from the fact that the women of the households in question do not get on well with their neighbors. The functioning of these clusters as social aggregates depends almost entirely on the women,

---

*Some individuals used the term masharakat to convey the social homogeneity of these clusters, but in a sense more adjectival than nominal, i.e. that close neighbors are good company, but not a company.

for it is they who activate the potential relationships. They wash clothes together at the well, they slip in and out of each other's houses, they gossip together while doing housework or preparing food, and they feel free to borrow each other's labor and utensils and cooking ingredients. Their children form play groups, often sharing a common sepak raga court and congregating beneath each other's houses, rarely playing with other "outside" children. The adult men of a cluster usually get on with each other—often they are close kinsmen—but much of their informal interaction is carried out in the coffee shop. It is the common kinship interests that provide the structural basis for these social clusters. Many of the women are "outsiders" (having married into the cluster) and are unrelated to each other, but have common interests in the behavior of their husbands (who often are related). In an indirect way, marital strains are often alleviated by the presence of sympathetic female neighbors who can give advice and comfort. The intimacy that exists helps to inhibit quarreling within a household, for the houses within a cluster are close together, and privacy is at a premium.

Some clusters are socially more coherent than others, and this is so particularly when the members have something distinctive in common. For example, one especially well-knit cluster includes a woman, her two married daughters, her son-in-law, grandchildren, and great-grandchildren, the children adopted by her daughter, her sister's daughter, and her husband and children. This cluster is of Minangkabau origin, and they are the only people of this bangsa in the village. They live in four houses, three of which are close together and the fourth about a quarter of a mile down the road. They see only each other and rarely, if ever, have anything to do with other members of the village. The three neighboring houses are separated from the next house by a fence of shrubs. Their extra-cluster contacts are almost exclusively with Minangkabau of Jendram Ulu and other villages and towns. It should, however, be noted that these clusters are purely social in import and are quite irrelevant to any sort of political alignment—they are to all intents and purposes aggregates of convenience almost exclusively domestically oriented and sharing in common such things as wells, mesin getah (mangles), and foot mortars (lesong indek), although other households may also use these things.

As already noted, kinship is one of the major underlying structural ties of social relations within these clusters, though the binding nature of kinship is greatly modified by the intensity of sentiment. The kinship ties of any and every Malay individual extend far beyond the cluster and the village. There is in fact no territorial boundary associated with geneal-ology, and the household and the cluster are the only units that can be de-fined geographically which have any coincidence with kinship ties. The jural and political significance of kinship is relatively minor and is for-malized in the rules and precepts of Islam, but kinship operating infor-mally is fundamental in providing a structural location for many of the most important social, moral, and sentimental values of the village Malay.

Some of the more formal structural aspects of Malay kinship, in-cluding the terminology, have been described by Djamour (1959), and what she says of Singapore Malays is applicable to the Malays of Jendram Hilir. There are certain differences, which will be described below, but my main concern is to convey some idea of the sociological role of kinship in the everyday life of villagers and to indicate the relationship between kinship statuses and social values.

Djamour says of the Singapore Malay that he: "seems to have a

-124-

particular dread of solitude, of being satu orang . . . . to be surrounded
by members of his family helps give the Malay a sense of security" (1959:
35). The same can be said of the Malays of Jendram Hilir, who express
the same sentiments and act in the same way. This explicit desire to be
surrounded by an emotional cocoon seems to be the major underlying ra-
tionale for the utilization and expression of kinship ties. Since kinship
ties are idealized as emotional ties, relations of intimacy and affection
between people not related by kinship are usually placed on a kinship basis.
Wherever possible, close relationships between people are incorporated
into an idiom of kinship, as this is the paradigm of human relations. All
relationships between people should preferably be personal, and the ideal
personal relation between two people is that which is supposed to exist between kin. Within the village, therefore, interaction between individuals
is predominantly between those who are kin to each other, and close relations between nonkin are, by and large, avoided. On the whole, these
networks of interpersonal relations are concentrated within the household
and household clusters described above.

Although kinship is a major feature of Malay village social life, the
hub of any set of relations is the individual, and the kinship group is not a
major feature of Malay village social structure. The village of Jendram
Hilir cannot be defined by any reference to the systematic arrangement of
kin ties within village boundaries. There is just one sense in which the majority of the village are unified, i.e. as opposing factions, with each faction being defined by reference to descent. This will be described more
fully below. The establishment of kin ties between persons and their definition to each other of their status within a specific context provide the
pattern by which the major tenets of interpersonal behavior may be specified.

Thus specific kin statuses may be said to denote not only a genealogical relationship but also an ideal pattern of interpersonal conduct, which includes both manner of acting and etiquette and expectations and responsibilities as well.

Kinship in general is denoted by the term saudara. This term can be extended metaphorically to include nonkin who hold each other in sufficient esteem and interact with sufficient frequency and intimacy to make their relationship as meaningful as if they were actually kin. As Djamour notes, "People who are not one's saudara are orang lain (strangers)" (1959: 24). Saudara is also a general term that describes "we" as opposed to "they" and implies solidarity. It is used in the village, for example, to describe all Malays as opposed to Chinese, although in another context, village Malays (orangorang kampong) may be described as Malays in opposition to urban Malays (orangorang bandar).

Whereas Singapore Malays distinguish saudara dekat (close kin) from saudara jauh (distant kin), the term keluarga is used in Jendram to denote close kin. This term also describes a kindred, a specific set of kinsmen related genealogically to one individual. It includes grandparents, parents, parents' siblings, cousins, siblings, children, nephews and nieces, and grandchildren. The term may also be extended to include any person regarded as being as emotionally close as keluarga (such as an adopted kinsman or a close friend). Conversely, a genealogical kinsman who is emotionally distant, although technically within the keluarga category, may not be considered keluarga, except on infrequent, purely formal occasions. Keluarga is a category of people of varying kinship status on whom an individual depends for close emotional support at all stages and events of his life. They are people with whom he expects to spend all of his life.

-126-

Keluarga are those people with whom "one's heart rests easy (hati senang)."

With but few exceptions, everyone in Jendram Hilir has keluarga resident in the village, mostly within the neighbor clusters. This is more true of men than of women, since many women have come into Jendram from elsewhere after marriage (which fact is offset in turn by the comparative frequency of marriage between kin). Especially after the birth of children, a woman becomes an integral part of her husband's keluarga, and it is the woman, more than the man, who activates social relations outside of the immediate household. Because of migration and marriage, most people also have keluarga living outside of the village. The social horizons of the villagers extend along individual lines out of the village and in some cases as far as Kelantan, Trengganu, Singapore, Ipoh, and Penang (though in the majority of cases, keluarga living outside of Jendram dwell within a three-hour traveling radius). These keluarga kindreds are activated by the extensive visiting patterns (jalanjalan) described above, and they may actually assemble as a congregation at various rituals undertaken by the focal individual—particularly at life cycle rituals. They are particularly important to the individual in times of illness or misfortune and at times of great joy.

At illness, death, and birth, the role of keluarga and the emotional meaning of the term are most clear-cut. To be alone during an illness or to have to cope single-handed with birth and death is unthinkable. The presence of one's keluarga at such times is mandatory, and it would seem that the hustle and bustle of an overcrowded household during the time of illness, birth, and death has a therapeutic effect on those most nearly affected by the event. The obligations, expectations, and responsibilities of being keluarga are paramount in Malay village thought about social relations—one not only expects to receive company and comfort during illness but one also expects to provide them during another's illness. The role of <u>keluarga</u> (more specifically defined by the particular kinship status pertaining between the individuals concerned) takes first priority in any hierarchy of values concerning interpersonal social relations.[*]

Within the household, irrespective of its actual composition, the paradigm of the relationship structure is the nuclear family. The father as head of the household is nominally dominant over the mother and children. Unless a grandparent is actually head of the household (i.e. owner of the house), he or she is subordinate in the actual conduct of household affairs, though genealogical seniority ensures a certain amount of respect which is made most explicit on formal occasions. Other relatives living in a household are arranged in status according to whether they are of the parental or filial generation with respect to the head and whether they are male or female. Formally, the female is of lower status than the male, but in the majority of households within the village, the woman dominates all phases of the running of the household and the conduct of social relations within it. In day-to-day decisions, such as what to buy and where, whether or not to tap rubber, and whether or not a particular task should be performed, the initiative is usually taken by the senior woman. The

---

[*]In interviews with a number of European employers of Malays in Kuala Lumpur, the alacrity with which Malay employees take off to visit a "sick uncle" was constantly cited as evidence of Malay irresponsibility and unsuitability for work—and hence in capacity for development. For the Malay, however, the fulfillment of his obligation to "visit a sick uncle" is a moral imperative which has only partial relationship to the severity of the illness and which certainly has priority over the fulfillment of the conditions of the formal relations between employer and employee. In the scheme of Malay values, the Malay who takes off under such circumstances is demonstrating his sense of responsibility rather than his lack of it.

disciplining of children is also carried out by the females with a secondary, somewhat formal, contribution by the male—unless he is the one immediately offended by the misconduct. Nominally women occupy an inferior status. They remain in the background, they stay in the back of the house, they take care never to be raised above the level of any man in the house, and in front of visitors they show much obsequiousness before their menfolk in, for example, serving coffee. When men gather together in a house to talk business, women sit in the back room and are rarely invited to give their opinion. But in fact they are constantly offering advice and suggestions, making pertinent (and impertinent) comments, and criticizing. Their opinions and counsel are often incorporated unconsciously into the decisions made by the men. In one case, for example, a girl was found with a boy in a rubber holding at dawn. The acting ketua kampong, the ketua kampong of Jendram Ulu, the imam, and the penghulu discussed the case throughout the night in the front of the house, while the women served coffee and sat in the back—but all the time the women were contributing to the discussion and imposing their own decision in the matter: that the two culprits should marry. Nominally, the man of the house has nothing to do with the kitchen, house cleaning, or care of the children, but in fact, when they are present in the house, Malay village fathers think nothing of giving a baby a bottle, cleaning up after children have defecated, clearing away dishes, and, in emergencies, cooking a meal.[*]

Formally then, the division between the sexes is quite explicit, with the women remaining in the background, never appearing in such public

---

[*]The only cooking said to be regularly done by men is preparing for Hari Raya Puasa a special cake (dodol) which requires constant stirring for at least five hours.

places as the coffee shop or mosque, and always appearing proper to the outside. Most of the women's social activities are conducted in the company of other women, and the men spend most of their time with each other. At midday and in the evening, men gather at the coffee shop and women sometimes gather in each other's houses. The younger men form peer groups, or geng, and spend most of the day with each other playing cards, talking, listening to the radio, or reading old newspapers and magazines. Adolescent girls look after children and the house and occasionally keep each other company—generally within the boundaries of the cluster. Preadolescent boys and girls often play with each other, though girls start to make an active contribution to the household when they are about six years old, thereby curtailing their time for play.

Within the household there is an approximate division of labor by sex and, to some extent, by age, with discipline and respect status correlated with generation. As a woman gets older she gradually assumes a status that is to all intents and purposes equal to that of her husband in all aspects, though the formal separation is still maintained (see above pp. 105-06).

Children are allowed considerable freedom of expression until they reach the age of about five or six years, when girls in particular assume minor household responsibilities, especially taking care of younger children. Corporal punishment is rarely administered, and then only by exceptional individuals who often bring upon themselves the censure of their neighbors. Sometimes children are pinched and pulled away roughly, but the principal disciplinary device is shaming (mendapat malu), most often by publicizing the misdemeanor to other members of the household or by threatening to do so, thereby embarrassing the child. The concept of malu is one that acts as a hidden thermostat in interpersonal social relations.

The term not only means shame, it also means shyness and embarrassment. For someone to be <u>malu</u> may be proper in the sense of being demure, but even demureness carries with it the implication that the status between two persons is unequal, and this is the core of the meaning of <u>malu</u>. That is to say, any diversion of the expectations of a relationship will result in <u>malu</u> or shame on the part of the one confounded and will also shame the one who makes the mistake. A graphic illustration of this concept occurred when a friend took me to meet his uncle. After the introduction, the conversation turned to the growing of corn. My friend's uncle made a joke to the effect that the only thing about corn as opposed to rice was that if you ate a lot of it, it built up wind in the stomach and this gave rise to especially loud passing of wind. He then pretended to illustrate. The host thought this very funny, but my friend was literally rendered speechless and put into a state of shock which lasted about three minutes. The host became very embarrassed and called for coffee, and as soon as possible we left. The crudeness of the behavior under the circumstances was such an acute embarrassment to my companion that he never, at least during the remainder of my stay, spoke to his uncle again. My companion also offered me the most abject apologies, in which he explained how shamed and embarrassed (<u>malu</u>) he was. This incident illustrates a number of other general features or values inherent in the Malay view of the conduct and matter of social relationships. One is that all relations, as statuses, are accompanied by mutual respect such that the needs of the other ideally should be anticipated. This consideration is always present, but is often hidden in especially close relations where the formal aspects of generation difference and so forth melt away, and members of different generations react to each other with great familiarity. The second quality illustrated is the idea of crudity and refinement, two concepts that provide the basis for categories of social value judgments made by village Malays.

Being correct, showing consideration and concern, anticipating the other, conducting oneself with gentleness and refinement, speaking softly and using the proper word, and, above all, being sensitive to the other person, all may be described by the term halus. This concept also is applied to inanimate things—a finely woven piece of cloth or a well-tempered blade, for example, may be described as halus. On the other hand, one who does not observe expected etiquette, who uses coarse language (e. g. calling a man jantan instead of lakilaki or a woman betina instead of perempuan), and above all one who proves himself insensitive is described by the term kasar. All people are classified as one or the other, and although there are many Malays who are kasar, all Malays are halus when compared to non-Malays, particularly Chinese, who are often unwittingly kasar.

Thus the constant standards of interpersonal relationships may be summed up as the sensitivity of each of the parties in a status to the other and the expectation of mutual sensitivity. Such sensitivity can only accompany relationships that are personal, and the personal relationship is probably the only relationship properly understood in the village. Certainly the idea that expectations and obligations of a human relationship may be governed by legal contract are alien: not even Islamic coding of conduct is given precedence over the propriety of conduct within the given situation as a mutual expression of oneself.

Although to be halus is the ideal, it is not necessarily the norm in the village: Malays often behave toward each other in manner that can only be classified as kasar, and a number of villagers, particularly Banjarese are typed as kasar. Classification into halus and kasar carries with it some implications of social status, for those who are halus are also thought of as being superior in certain ways. Thus members of the aristocracy are almost by definition halus, although the villagers who claim entitlement to use the title "Raja" are accorded no different status than any other villager (in fact, it is claimed, their titles are valid only in Sumatra and not in Malaya). However, the titles Raja and Wak seem to carry with them a certain amount of nostalgia for those who claim them.

Individual status differentiation within the village is based on two factors, one of which is seen as a manifestation of the other. The basic factor may be distilled as the concept of pandai or skill. Pandai is applied to a person or to an act characterized by finesse and perfection. A person who is pandai, whether it be at carpentry, games, story-telling, rubber tapping, cooking, or dressmaking, is one who performs the task as well as can be expected and therefore better than others, although the definition is not a comparative one in the sense of implying competition. Likewise, any particular act—an argument, a Koran reading, securing a bargain, etc. — which is performed to complete satisfaction merits the compliment pandai for the performer. Standards of measurement are not absolute, but are relative in that the better performer may be recognized as pandai, even though by any absolute standard he may not be so. Unless a woman is able to cook exactly to the taste of her husband, she may not be described as pandai, even though to another she may seem to be a superb cook. To be pandai as a person is to merit consistent esteem and respect. As a performer, it may be as the result of a single act. To be esteemed by one's fellows is a mark of status, but not a formal one, for it pertains only to individuals and is not passed on. It provides no basis for any sort of stratification within the village. There are, on the other hand, certain statuses or offices which are almost always filled in the village and which do carry with them esteem—in order to occupy them their incumbents must ipso facto be pandai. Chief of these is the office of imam, and included also are the other mosque officials—the bilal (caller to prayer), guru (religious teacher), and khatib (reciter). Schoolmasters also enjoy esteem, but since they are so often outsiders, only temporarily resident in the village, they are not always able to exercise the influence that could stem from their roles. Somewhat more variable in the esteem accompanying it is the office of ketua kampong, an office that is bound to the formality of government. More generally speaking, skills such as literacy are highly esteemed, though one who is literate does not necessarily earn a particularly advantageous status. Since the quality is one that is diffused throughout the community, and is held in some way or other by virtually everyone, no single person is elevated above any other into a social station, but the influence of those who are pandai within their particular activities is greater than those who are not skilled. The converse of pandai is bodoh (clumsy or stupid). Used in a social sense it is somewhat similar to kasar but carries far more connotation of inferiority and is more usually applied to the bungling of specific acts, rather than to describe the total personality or accomplishments of an individual.

Wealth is viewed as accruing from the possession of superior talents, i.e. as a manifestation of pandai, and although rich men (orangorang kaya) may be materially better off than other villagers, they are not necessarily envied, nor is their total social personality removed from the matrix of village social relations. But the term does have two shades of meaning. It is used as a compliment when applied to those orangorang kaya in the village who are pandai and halus, who are generous in that they employ coolies, and who help their kinsmen. If orangorang kaya interact with other villagers as if they were no wealthier than anyone else, they receive the esteem that they think to be their due. But if there is any conscious effort at exclusiveness or any evidence of not being halus in social relations, then orangorang kaya may be used in a derogatory sense, as it is when it is applied to the urban wealthy and to members of other bangsa— such as Chinese.

Orangorang miskin may also be used of people in two senses. In one sense it may describe those villagers who are economically poor and who must live frugally, but who interact with others as social equals. For example, there is in the village a very poor family who make just about enough to live on, but the male head has made the pilgrimage to Mecca (having been taken by his grandfather) and is therefore qualified to be called "Haji." He and his family enjoy absolute freedom to go in and out of the house of orangorang kaya, with whom they enjoy social relations as equals. This contrasts with the second sense of the concept, which describes families whose poverty represents a lack of basic social qualification, or those families who are not only poor but also vulgar (kasar) and stupid (bodoh). Such families are not welcome in the houses of other villagers and would not attempt to enter them, even on occasions when they might be expected to—such as during Hari Raya Puasa. Occasionally orangorang miskin kasar do come to visit, but they are accorded the minimum of hospitality and their behavior is taken as evidence of their crudeness. A number of the households described in general as miskin (implying kasar) within the village include those of different bangsa, particularly the Banjarese households.

Those who have made the pilgrimage to Mecca, and who may therefore be addressed as Haji, enjoy only a limited prestige in the village unless they may also be described as pandai in some aspect of Islam. There
are, for example, two young men who may be addressed as Haji who are
in fact barely conversant with the Koran and whose behavior is most im-
pious. They had been taken to Mecca by their father and so had not saved
up themselves for the pilgrimage. They garner little or no esteem in the
village.

Although status distinctions based on wealth and skill within the village are evident, they are not formalized and they do not qualify their
incumbents for exclusive social interaction such that all those who may be
described as orangorang kaya may be said to form a social stratum. The
focus is entirely on the individual and extends at the most to the household. Status in the more formal sense becomes significant only when the
reference extends beyond the village—that is to say, when the Malay social system is taken to include professional Malays, especially schoolteachers, and the penghulu and other bureaucratic officials.

The major distinguishing factor is education. The possession of an
education creates common bonds of social preference between the educated and puts up barriers between those who are and those who are not
educated. Since life in the village has very little to do with such matters,
status based on education is relevant primarily to the analysis of urban Malay social structure. But since schoolmasters and lower officials do live in
or near the village, their social status does impinge on the social life of
the village—though mainly in a negative sense. Although the penghulu
and, to a lesser extent, the schoolmasters attempt to come close to the
villagers, their interests and values derived from their education tend to

separarate them socially. They visit village homes, but are received only in a formal way, and they come only with business in mind. The penghulu is consistently criticized throughout the village for never calling a meeting to discuss affairs, for never spending any time with village people, for always being somewhat abrupt, and for spending so much of his time in the district office—in other words, for being distant and impersonal. Schoolteachers are potentially of considerable influence in a village, for they are usually the most sophisticated people living there, are familiar with the bureaucratic process, and often have personal contacts in government offices. They can, therefore, be of great help to villagers and can initiate much social change even though they may reside for only a few years in the village and therefore have to overcome the disadvantage during that time of being an outsider. The status separation may still be apparent even when a schoolmaster has the confidence and cooperation of the village. This is the case in the neighboring village of Sungei Marab, where the schoolmaster in effect leads a double life—one in the village, where he visits villagers informally, and the other in Kajang, where he enjoys the company of his peers. In Jendram, both schoolteachers are newly resident in the village, though both have been teaching at the school for several years. The headmaster and his wife detest village living and take every opportunity to spend their free time with their friends in Seremban. The status gap between them and the villagers is wide. The other teacher, after moving into the village, turned increasingly to the company of villagers for his social activities and appeared to be well on the way to becoming an integral part of the social network of the village. His superior education and skills, coupled with acceptance into the social life of some of the village families, may well lead to his becoming an influential voice in affairs affecting the village. Mention has already been made of the adult schoolteacher who was born and bred in the village and who has had a secondary school education. His status in the village deserves some description. On the one hand, he is young (twenty-two years old) and unmarried and spends a lot of his time with the geng, who while away the days playing cards, listening to the radio, and so on. This tends to reduce his prestige among many of the elder villagers. On the other hand, he is able to read and write in both Malay scripts and he keeps reasonably well abreast of local affairs. It is he who drafts and writes petitions and letters for villagers, and, by virtue of his greater knowledge of the bureaucratic process, it is his opinion and advice that is often followed by others in approaching government officers and in taking action on affairs of mutual interest. These special qualifications give him a quite distinctive status in many spheres of social life in the village, particularly the political.

Jendram Hilir is not a politically active village, either in the sense of any sort of participation in national politics through the local UMNO cell or in a local sense, wherein villagers concern themselves with public projects or show interest in local plans. In the few events that may be characterized as political, in which members of the village participate in a decision-making process on affairs of public import, a social structure becomes apparent that is not without some interest. This has been described elsewhere (Wilson 1966) and will only be cursorily examined here.

The major bangsa of the village are Mandiling, Ramba, and Kepunohan. Each bangsa claims its unity and loyalty by reference to common descent through males. The aggregate so defined is called keterunan, a term which also applies to the five-generation span of Malay kinship

-138-

terminology. The Ramba and Kepunohan keterunan are actually descended from two brothers who married two sisters, and their aggregation may therefore be traced matrilineally as well. When this is done, the structural unit is called by villagers a suku (the same term used in Negri Sembilan to describe the matrilineage). Since the Mandiling living in the village are also descended from a common ancestor, they also use the term keterunan, although in the actual genealogy the descent is bilateral. The sole purpose of invoking descent is to provide a basis for clarification of the major factions in the village which oppose each other on matters political. The division in the village is reflected in geography as well, in that the Ramba-Kepunohan coalition lives in the main part of the village and the Mandiling live in a section between the 27th and 28th milestones. The latter are the newcomers, and they have succeeded better economically and socially, having sent a number of their members to secondary school. At the time of field work, the acting village headman, appointed by the penghulu, was Mandiling. The opposition is also reflected in the fact that the Indian-owned coffee shop in the village is frequented mostly by Mandiling, while the Malay-owned coffee shop is used by the other faction.

At the time of field work, there was an alliance between the Mandiling (represented by the acting headman) and the administration, represented by the penghulu, which alliance was opposed by the Ramba-Kepunohan coalition. The following incident occurred in which the factionalism became apparent: The headman and the penghulu proposed that the path to the cemetery be cleared and tidied up by volunteers. They were opposed with the argument (somewhat specious) that such work should be carried out for the village by the Public Works Department. On the day appointed for clearing, no one of the opposition appeared. When the penghulu asked that the area around the balai rayat (village hall) be cleared of brush and scrub, only the headman, his son, and a friend turned up for the work.

The Ramba-Kepunohan alliance is for all practical purposes composed of a small committee of elders, known as the rumpun, which also includes certain influential villagers such as the imam, the bilal, the khatib, and the adult schoolteacher (cf. Gullick 1958: 37: "The elders (ketua-tuaan) took part in the discussion of village affairs and negotiated the settlement of quarrels and disputes between their respective groups"). It is they who seek to determine what shall be done in the village, if anything, and they try to bypass the official authority of the acting ketua kampong and the penghulu. This is done by addressing their requests directly to the Mentri Besar of Selangor instead of going through the penghulu and the district office. Thus when they became dissatisfied with the design of the village mosque and wanted some modifications made, they decided to apply to the Mentri Besar. On another occasion I was present at a meeting of the rumpun at which they decided to make a direct request for piped water in order to forestall the penghulu, who they already knew was trying to get this done. At the very same meeting, they decided to oppose the suggestion that electricity be brought to the village. There is a deadlock concerning the appointment of a new ketua kampong. The Ramba-Kepunohan coalition has proposed two candidates, and the present acting ketua kampong has also been proposed with the backing of the penghulu. The alliance has periodically filed complaints to the Mentri Besar's office against the acting headman and the penghulu, and as a result of the total situation the appointment has been hanging fire for two years.

-140-

This factionalism, it must be emphasized, is exclusively political, and politics is unimportant in the village. It does not impinge greatly on village social life, and it concerns only the men. There is a slight carry-over in that ceremonial functions within the village are surreptitiously exclusive along faction lines, although openly everyone is invited. The mosque committee is dominated by the alliance, and one or two Mandiling attend Friday prayers at the mosque in Jendram Ulu because of this. In part it may be argued that the very existence of this faction is the reason that it plays so inactive a part in the projects and decisions of mutual or public interest to the village, which are kept to an absolute minimum so as not to disturb the ideal of calm social relations. The more scope provided for disagreement, the more pronounced the factions are likely to become, and the greater the departure from the ideal. Something of this order seems to account for the claims made by the penghulu, and admitted by some of the villagers themselves, that Jendram Hilir is completely apathetic as regards to initiative or change.

Apart from those mentioned above, the only formal statuses in the village are the religious offices of imam, bilal, and khatib. These are men who, relative to others in the village, display skill in Islam and earn esteem. The imam of Jendram enjoys considerable esteem because he is of extremely scholarly bent, has spent eighteen years living in Mecca, and is therefore very fluent in Arabic. Fluency in Arabic and acquaintance and knowledge of Arabic culture is in itself very prestigious. However, the imam is rather retiring and has considerable interests in land outside of the village, so that he plays a relatively small part in the lives of the villagers outside of the affairs of the mosque (unlike the imam of Jendram Ulu, who though by no means as accomplished a scholar, is a

-141-

most active advisor to the community). Some of the moral guidance functions of the imam are exercised by the bilal and the khatib, both of whom
are Haji and reasonably proficient in Arabic and the Koran and Islamic law.

Islam provides the over-all, formal design for Malay village life,
while adat and mutual convenience mold actual everyday conduct and
values. The formal acts of Islam—praying five times a day, abstaining
from pork, attending mosque on a Friday, observing the major religious
festivals (especially the fast of Ramadan), learning the Koran, and dress-
ing properly—all these are observed with consistency throughout the village. The formal separation of the sexes and the superficially inferior
status of women are also manifestations of the influence of Islamic values.
But the day-to-day regulation of interaction and its underlying values de-
pend on adat and on practical considerations. Thus gambling and lotter-
ies are frowned on by Islam but practiced in the village; fasting is mandatory during Ramadan, even enforced by police action, but the fast is often
broken by a large number of individuals (cf. Djamour 1959: 15: "only a
small proportion [of Singapore Malays] fasted the whole month [of Rama-
dan])." Although women should be modestly dressed at all times, it has
been noted above that older women often are very relaxed in their own
homes. The independence and influence of women is another manifestation of the village departure from the formal governance of Islam. Even
such formal prescriptions as praying five times a day and attending mosque
regularly on Friday are not always observed in their entirety by all villagers, who act with more flexibility than they may say they do.

The influence of religious values in everyday life and the influence
of some of the adat value concepts outlined above, such as halus and
kasar, can be conveyed more clearly if the distinction between the public

and the private domain in Malay life is recognized.

The private domain includes the behavior of Malays within the confines of their own homes (such as the partial undress of women), the behavior of Malays with close and intimate members of their families (when conversation may well include innuendos, jokes, and remarks that in any other context would be considered most unbecoming or kasar), and the behavior of Malays among themselves as distinct from any outsider. It may also include behavior between men, as in a coffee shop for example. In the private domain, the formal observance of values, standards, and niceties is relaxed and people take their cues from each other and as the moment dictates. The public domain, on the other hand, involves behavior on view to outsiders, these being defined relative to the specific situation. Thus a woman must be properly dressed when exposed to anyone not a member of her household; when nonkinsmen or unfamiliar kinsmen gather, they should observe the niceties of interpersonal behavior—they should be halus. Publicly, the Malay male has a higher "status" than the female, but privately this may not be so. Publicly, differences of wealth may contribute to social differentiation, but privately these may be irrelevant. In the same way, religion is formally important in the public domain, but, with the exception of a few devout individuals, Islam is relatively unimportant in the private domain. This is not to say that any outsider can therefore proceed to attack or attempt to modify these public standards, for these are the reality for the Malay relative to the outsider. Even if a Malay villager regularly breaks the fast of Ramadan by smoking each day in the back of the coffee shop, he is still a devout Moslem when compared to any outsider. Even though women may work around the house bare from the waist up, the acceptance of Western dress—immodest by comparison with the Malay dress—is by no means possible, because publicly the standard prescribes Malay dress.

Social interaction in the village cannot easily be boiled down to the acting out of an underlying structure. But there are certain regularities between people of a structural nature, especially kin ties. If there is a unit of social organization, it is the household, between whose members there exists binding ties of kinship. But ties of kinship extend beyond any territorial unit. The manner of interpersonal behavior is quite definitely modulated by adherence to a set of commonly held values concerning respect, esteem, sensitivity, and skill. The relevance of these values to social behavior is modified by the relativity of the public and private domain. This also tends to modify the rigidity of ritual behavior, which is based on a code that originates outside the scope of village relations, principally in Islam. Other manifestations of structural qualities—descent aggregates and social status—come about only in response to events of limited social reference and relevance. Such statuses as pawang (shaman), for example, are activated so seldom in the village that with the death of the present incumbent the status itself is likely to vanish.

CONCLUSION

The village of Jendram Hilir, Selangor, is as typical as any one village can be of villages on the west coast of Malaya dependent on rubber tapping for a livelihood. This does not, however, make it a typical Malay village, for there are many variants of these. The most striking feature of a village such as this is the lack of sociological unity—the village is a unit only in certain designated spheres, mostly imposed from outside, either by the administration or as a religious unit. Put in another way, social life in the village revolves around the individual and small clusters of individuals, such as households. The networks of social relations in which village individuals are placed spread beyond the village, and relations within the village are more incidental than structured. This generalization should be modified somewhat in that coresidence and inheritance make for a certain amount of concentration of village social relations, some of which are based on kinship and others on friendship. The specific conditions of the founding of the village and the presence of factions which define themselves by criteria of descent are perhaps a little exceptional, but the existence and the use of such concepts of descent suggest that they may be more general than has hitherto been reported.

When the center and initiator of social relations is the individual rather than the group, and when the role positions in any one network reach out more or less at random beyond the coresidential unit, it is not too much to expect that relations are activated with respect to mutual, individual interest and that corporate interests will receive little if any sympathy. In rendering the pattern of Malay social relations into a structural vocabulary, one can describe them as being fundamentally dyadic, where each event necessitating a relationship is treated in isolation and where the status positions with respect to any one individual can only be linked together through that individual. This seems to be a general feature of bilaterally organized kinship systems and consequently of societies in which bilateral kinship provides a basic plan for the structure of social relations. A similar position is taken by Jay in his unpublished paper (1964) dealing with local politics in Perak.

In establishing the structural nature of social relations among rural Malays one must make explicit the ideological level of social relations. By this I mean the less tangible level of values and emotions. The idiom of social relations is expressed in kinship—kinship relations not only provide the greatest number of actual status and role positions but they also provide the basis for the moral and cultural views held by Malays about interpersonal relationships in general. Any formulation of these values is necessarily imprecise, but certain tenets can be stated with some decisiveness. All relationships should be established at a personal level. The implications of this tenet are that the successful fulfillment of any task cannot be expected unless the Malay party is quite certain of his role and is satisfied in his expectations from the other party. Each and every relationship is mutual and involves the fulfillment of emotional as well as more

-146-

formal expectations. The actual status levels may be unequal, but so long as they are defined and the expectations of each rendered, the relationship can be smooth. The paradigm of social relations is the kinship system where status is clearly marked, but where there are not only functional expectations but emotional ones as well. Since all relations are mutual and reciprocal, the exact nature of the reciprocity should be reasonably well specified, and this is the main function of the system of etiquette. Etiquette provides the formal means of expressing the mutual respect of one relationship position to the other and thereby ensuring a proper functioning of that relationship. Etiquette not only means entering a house properly, it means the use of a proper vocabulary, consciousness of the other's moods and needs, the extension of hospitality and the desire to accept it, and the many other small ways of showing mutual respect. All of these ways are specifically defined and learned with respect to kinship and are extended by analogy to nonkinship relations.[*]

For these reasons and because this pattern seems to be so unalterably a part of Malay village culture, relations between villagers and non-Malays are difficult to pursue satisfactorily unless the outsider can fulfill the Malay expectations of the role in which he is defined. To achieve the fulfillment, the outsider must be aware of what is expected and be willing to provide it. But the relations with outsiders are invariably formal, not reciprocal or personal. They are satisfied by the Malay according

---

[*] It should not be inferred from this that all kinship relations among village Malays are marked by absolute harmony. The friction that does occur, however, is a "private matter," hidden from those not involved (i.e. the outsider).

to his definition of the situation in which he provides the behavior he con-
siders is required, and often this anticipation of requirements is based only
on the consideration of the other role as a person and not an office. That
is to say, all relationships as far as Malay villagers are concerned are
human relationships, and have as a minimum requirement a mutual sensitivity of mood and understanding. The paradigm on which such expectations are based is the set of kinship relations in which every Malay is placed.
The sanctions are inherent in the relation and are moral in nature, instead
of being external to the relations and upheld by a code of law. In a relationship that involves persons acting as representatives of an office (headman, district officer, clerk, foreman, manager) both the definition of
the role and its content and its sanction are fundamentally legal and rest
squarely on the idea and validity of legal contract. Mood, sentiment,
and feeling are irrelevant; obligations are framed and defined with reference to codes which in their turn come to have a legitimacy of their
own, independent of all time and circumstance. If it says in the book
that a man must pay taxes or register his name, then he must—because it
says so in the book. The officer goes by the book. Similarly the organization of Western business and industry rests firmly on the concept of
legal contract: the relation between employer and employee is not a personal one, but is bound by mutual obligation incurred by recognition of
a legal contract. There is nothing of this in Malay village values—obligations inhere within specific relations between persons with a social, as
opposed to a bureaucratic, identity. Consequently, the village Malay
acts according to the values he learns as a participant in traditional social
relations even when brought into contact with outsiders. The outsider,
the developer, acts according to "values" anchored ultimately in a legal
contract.

-148-

Unless and until a villager understands the idea of legal contract and can come to value it in the same way as the outsider, the one will continue to misunderstand the other. The relationship between "status" and "contract" to social change was pointed out long ago in Maine's Ancient Law, and was elaborated with great precision and thoroughness by Max Weber, although their starting points were a little different. Their insights, however, seem to have remained confined to the classroom and theory.

If this basic point of difference between villager and "developer" is in any way accurate, it becomes easier to understand the occurrence and the importance of what is termed "paternalism" as an unsystematic but widespread attempt to close the gap between two systems of values: one, the bureaucratic, rational Western system of contract, the other the traditional, personal status system. One is legal, the other moral. Going on from there, one is tempted to observe that "planned development," if it is to follow "Western" lines, should include, at an early stage, an explanation, translation, definition, and inculcation of the idea of contract for the benefit of those to be "developed."

The basic value system of social relations and the conditions of contact with outsiders are such that the latter become stereotypes, and the feedback of village experience with outsiders seen as stereotypes tends only to ratify the system and make it less flexible. The limited information about the other ethnic groups of Malaya and other outsiders, as well as national and international events and processes, further restricts the ability of villagers to take the initiative to comprehend, care about, or feel the need to alter their roles in their own life situations. But having made such a generalization, it is necessary to note the exceptions. With some approach to accuracy, it can be said that the age group above forty is less adjusted to change and the outside than those under forty, and with less certainty it can be ventured that women are more flexible in outlook than men and in the village context more responsible for what changes do occur. In part this may be due to the dominance of the house and household in Malay life and to the fact that the woman dominates the household in all but the ceremonial aspects.

The economic position of the people of the village is by and large comfortable (bearing in mind that any measurement is strictly relative). Food and the purchasing power for food is sufficient, and other material needs can be satisfied, though there are considerable differences among households in this respect. Overwhelming problems of debt are absent, and the possibility of catastrophe seems remote to the villagers—rubber produces a steady income each day. The long-term prospects are not bright, since the majority of the trees are coming to the end of their productive lives and little is being done in advance to prepare for this. The village has neither electricity nor piped water, and it is possible that if and when these are introduced the demand for apparatus and gadgets will have a major adverse effect on the sufficiency of income. A number of children, both boys and girls, attend the secondary school in Kajang, and there is a general recognition throughout the village that education is worthwhile. But those who receive this education will, with but few exceptions, leave the village to work in offices in the larger towns, leaving those with only the minimum education and those with the least abilities to remain in the village as the undeveloped rural masses. Their daily lives and their livelihood will be earned according to the methods and precepts they have learned in the village, mainly in the household, which means that little change is likely. I believe that this process is as basic to any form of development as questions of mechanization, industrialization, and so forth. The approach to the solution of this problem lies first in the understanding of the basic tenets and structure of village life and then in the formulation of a means of effective communication of concepts, methods, and values, as well as techniques and the supply of material on which the entire process of change and development rests. I am in effect arguing for a translation of nonvillage values into a set of concepts comprehensible to villagers. Put in another way, the prerequisite for change is a presentation of the anthropology of the societies from which the changes emanate. Thus the values associated with "work" in a capitalist or even in a socialist economy are not only different from the values about work in a Malay village but are integrated in, and help to integrate, a total social structure that is different.

I do not intend to launch into this argument too far, but a suggestion as to how values and concepts of change can be conveyed may be in order. Briefly, the curriculum of the village school, instead of being adjusted to secondary education, might be adjusted to the demands of changing village life and aimed at those who will continue to live in the village, rather than those who will leave for the towns. The learning process, if looked at as an exercise in translation, should also be modified and be brought more into line with the traditional education process carried out in the home. Here the degree of abstraction is kept to a minimum, explanation is by demonstration and by trial and error, mediation through the printed word or picture is almost nonexistent—one learns to fish by fishing, not by reading about it, and to tap rubber by tapping rather than with printed instructions. *

In sum, the object of this report is to convey to the interested general reader the nature of those values underlying social life in a Malay village which most nearly touch on the problems of change and development. It will be noted that religion is all but omitted in the above account. This is not to deny the importance of Islam, either in the direction of daily life or in the provision of a broad plan for the morality of life. For one thing, the precise injunctions and values stressed by Islam can be read in other sources, but a more important reason for the lack of detailed treatment is that apart from the observance of certain of the technical requirements of the religion (fasting, praying, abstinence), Islam plays little part in the values of day-to-day interaction in Jendram Hilir. In this respect the village may be exceptional, but this remains to be seen. Islam is a prestige possession for villagers when they contrast themselves with outsiders, particularly Chinese, and such facets as knowledge of Arabic and Jawi script are prized as much for their "oneupmanship" value over Chinese as for their intrinsic aesthetic and religious importance. On the other hand, no outsider should underestimate the emotional significance of Islam to village Malays, nor to any Malay for that matter, and Islam is frequently used as a rallying point by Malay politicians for national unity and international alliances.

The choice of village Malay values as a topic for this report is based

---

* This argument supports, from an anthropological standpoint, Schultz's convincing economic argument for the priority of the development of education, particularly at the primary level, in underdeveloped countries (Schultz 1964, especially chapter 12).

on the contention that vague and intangible as they are, values are a fundamental factor in the total process of social, cultural, and technical change, and that in spite of this, they are too little considered in theses on the question of change. It is also implied that any discussion of change or development at the national level, whether it be political, economic, or otherwise, must fundamentally relate to that sector of the population which is undeveloped, namely the rural masses, the villagers. Finally, it should be pointed out that this report aims only at being a synchronic study of the relationship of the villagers of Jendram Hilir to their outside world at the time of field work—September 1964 to April 1965.

Glossary of Colloquial Malay Terms Used in Text

adat custom, customary law; adat betul, authentic culture; adat
perpateh, matrilineal law

bagi dua to "go halves" in an economic transaction

balai rayat village (literally peoples') hall

bandar urban

bangsa an ethnic aggregate, but more broadly any culturally homo-
geneous group

beli buy, used in phrase pandai beli - well bought

beras husked but uncooked rice

bersilat the traditional Malay fencing, but also a dance based on the
sport

bersunat circumcision

betina female of animals, plants; vulgar term for humans

bidan midwife

bilal muezzin of a mosque; one who calls believers to prayer

biken duit to make or earn money

belachan shrimp paste

bodoh stupid, also used in the sense of bumpkin

bomoh village healer

chari wang to earn money, to seek to earn money

chuka formic acid used to coagulate latex

daerah an administrative district

dekat close, near, used in phrase saudara dekat, close kin

demam a fever; a term used in general to indicate illness accompanied
by a temperature change

dodol a taffylike sweetmeat made only at Hari Raya Puasa and cooked
by men—ingredients include sugar, grated coconut, and coconut milk
and glutinous rice

-154-

dusun   an orchard, but also used to describe any group of fruit trees

geng   a peer group of young unmarried men

getah   rubber; getah puteh, good quality raw rubber; getah buku, lumps of poor quality rubber picked up from the base of the tree

gotong royong   the institution of reciprocal, cooperative labor known but not practiced—better known as a Javanese institution

gunting rambut   haircut, but specifically the ritual of a child's first haircut

guru   a teacher, particularly a religious teacher, colloquially termed che'gu

haj   the pilgrimage to Mecca

Haji   the title used by one who has made the pilgrimage

halus   refined, proper

Hari Raya Puasa   the month of celebration following the fast of Ramadan

harta   property, but particularly that designated in adat as being heritable (harta pusaka)

hatam koran   the celebration following the completion of a child's Koranic studies - often held as a joint feast with circumcision

hati senang   literally an easy liver, meaning contentment

ikan bilis   small dried fish of piquant flavor

imam   head of the mosque

jalanjalan   to wander at leisure; to visit socially

jantan   male of animals, plants; vulgar term for humans

jauh   far, distant; used in phrase saudara jauh, distant kin

Jawi   Arabic script

kampong   village, hamlet, and also, in a general sense, rural

kasar   coarse, crude

kati   measure, the equivalent of one and one third pounds

kaya   wealthy

kawan   friend

kebon   a garden, but used occasionally to describe a rubber holding and, more generally, any planted area

keluarga   family, close kin

kendury   a feast or celebration; also any party

keping   a slice or sheet; keping getah puteh, a rubber sheet

kerbau   water buffalo

kerja   work; kerja bersamasama, literally to work together, a cooperative work group

keterunan   the five-generation span of Malay kinship terminology and used to denote a patrilineal descent aggregate

ketua kampong   village headman
khatib   reciter, a reader in the mosque
kotor   dirty and also impure
kuli   menial laborer
ladang   a dry-rice field; also a rubber estate
lakilaki   male
lalang   long, rough grass or weeds
lauk   side dishes, served with rice at every meal
lesong indek   a mortar worked by foot
makan gaji   to earn wages
malu   shyness, shame, embarrassment
masharakat   a business company, but also used to indicate any group
    with active common interests, especially economic
mendapat malu   shaming as a means of discipline
mesin getah   mangles
miskin   poor
mukim   a subdistrict or parish
orang   person; orang lain, stranger; orang orang, people; orang puteh,
    white man
padi   rice on the stalk; padi bukit literally hill rice, but actually dry rice
panas   hot as of temperature
pandai   clever, skilled, expert; pandai beli, well bought
parang   broad-bladed knife similar to a machete
pawang   magician, but also a ritual officiant
pedas   hot, in the sense of peppery
penghulu   government appointed official administrating a mukim
perempuan   female
pondok   a shelter, especially in rice fields, orchards, or by the road
pulut   glutinous rice
puteh   white; orang puteh, white man
Ramadan   the Moslem month of fasting
rayat   subject class, also population
rezeki   food, but also the idea of economic fate, one's determined
    allotment
Rumi   Roman script
rumpun   a root or a clump, a numeral coefficient for grasses; also used
    to designate the inner group of elders in the village
sambal   condiment, especially one that includes chili pepper
saudara   kin; saudara dekat, close kin; saudara jauh, distant kin
sawah   padi field

sayor   vegetables

sekolah   school; sekolah kebangsaan, national primary school

semangat   spirit

sepak raga   Malay national game played by two teams of three players
    each using feet, hands, and head to propel a rattan ball over a net
    but within a court

sireh   the leaf of the betel vine; the betel quid

sisa   leftovers, remains

sudu   ladle, also the small spout for channeling rubber latex into the cup

songkok   customary male hat

suku   a quarter; also a matrilineally defined aggregate

surau   a building used for prayer when no mosque is available

susu   milk, also rubber latex

tempat getah   the place where rubber latex is coagulated and rolled into
    sheets

tempat sireh   special betel sets

tikar   mat

tolong menolong   reciprocal help

towkay   a Chinese merchant, but also applied to a Malay or Indian
    merchant

tuai   a special knife used only to cut padi stem by stem

wakil   an agent; wakil pos, postal agent

waliah   religious district

wangi   fragrant, also delicate of flavor

BIBLIOGRAPHY

Aziz, Ungku A.
1964   Poverty and rural development in Malaysia. Kajian
         Ekonomi Malaysia 1: 70-105.

Brackman, Arnold C.
1966   Southeast Asia's second front. New York, Frederick A.
         Praeger.

Burling, Robbins
1965   Hill farms and padi fields: life in mainland Southeast
         Asia. Englewood Cliffs, Prentice-Hall, Inc.

Djamour, Judith
1959   Malay kinship and marriage in Singapore. London School
         of Economics, Monographs on Social Anthropology 21.

Dobby, E. H. G. et al.
1955   Padi landscapes of Malaya. Malayan Journal of Tropical
         Geography 6 /whole volume/.

1957   Padi landscapes of Malaya. Malayan Journal of Tropical
         Geography 10 /whole volume/.

Firth, Raymond
1946   Malay fishermen: their peasant economy. London, Kegan
         Paul, Trench, Trubner, and Co.

Firth, Rosemary
    1943   Housekeeping among Malay peasants. London School of
                Economics, Monographs on Social Anthropology 7.

Fisher, C. A.
    1956   The problem of Malayan unity in its geographical setting.
                In Geographical Essays on British Tropical Lands, R. W.
                Steel and C. A. Fisher, eds. London, George Philip &
                Son, Ltd. Pp. 269-344.

Fisk, E. K.
    1963   Features of the rural economy. In The Political Economy
                of Independent Malaya, Thomas H. Silcock and E. K.
                Fish, eds. Berkeley, University of California Press. Pp.
                163-73.

Freedman, Maurice
    1957   Chinese family and marriage in Singapore. Colonial Re-
                search Studies 20. London.

    1959   The handling of money: a note on the background to the
                economic sophistication of overseas Chinese. Man 59:
                64-65.

Ginsburg, Norton and Chester F. Roberts, Jr.
    1958   Malaya. Seattle, University of Washington Press.

Gullick, John Michael
    1955   Kuala Lumpur, 1880-1895. Journal of the Malayan Branch
                of the Royal Asiatic Society 28 Part 4, No. 172 /whole
                issue/.

    1958   Indigenous political systems of western Malaya. London
                School of Economics, Monographs on Social Anthropology
                17.

Hall, D. G. E.
    1955   A history of Southeast Asia. London, Macmillan and Co.,
                Ltd.

Jackson, R. N.
    1961   Immigrant labour and the development of Malaya, 1786-
             1920. Kuala Lumpur, Government Press.

Jay, R.
    1964   Local and national politics in a rural Malay community.
             Paper read at the Association for Asian Studies Annual
             Meeting, Washington 1964.

LeBar, Frank M., Gerald C. Hickey, and John K. Musgrave
    1964   Ethnic groups of mainland Southeast Asia. New Haven,
             HRAF Press.

Netto, George
    1961   Indians in Malaya. Singapore, published by the author.

Purcell, Victor
    1948   The Chinese in Malaya. London, Oxford University Press.

Puthucheary, J. J.
    1960   Ownership and control in the Malayan economy. Singapore,
             published by D. Moore for Eastern Universities Press.

Schultz, Theodore W.
    1964   Transforming traditional agriculture. New Haven, Yale
             University Press.

Sendut, Hamzah
    1962   Patterns of urbanization in Malaya. Journal of Tropical
             Geography 16: 114-30.

Swift, M. G.
    1963   Capital, saving and credit in a Malay peasant economy.
             In Capital, Saving and Credit in Peasant Societies,
             Raymond Firth and B. S. Yamey, eds. London, George
             Allen & Unwin, Ltd.

    1965   Malay peasant society in Jelebu. London School of Eco-
             nomics, Monographs on Social Anthropology 29.

Tjoa, Soei Hock
  1963   Institutional background to modern economic and social
            development in Malaya. Kuala Lumpur, Liu & Liu.

Wilson, Peter J.
  1966   A note on descent in a Malay village. Behavior Science
            Notes 1: 7-13.

Winstedt, Richard
  1950   The Malays: a cultural history. Revised ed. London,
            Routledge & Kegan Paul, Ltd.

Wolff, R. J.
  1963   A comparison of cultural patterns of the Malays and the
            aborigines as they relate to health problems. Unpublished
            manuscript.

Official Publications Cited:

Malaysia Federation.
  1960   Monthly Statistical Bulletin, December. Kuala Lumpur.

  1962   Report on employment, unemployment and underemploy-
            ment. Kuala Lumpur.

  1963   Official Year Book /Buku Rasmi Tahunan/. Vol. 3.
            Kuala Lumpur.

INDEX

aborigine peoples, 4
acculturation, 39 ff.
Achehnese, 8
adat, vii, 7, 22, 45, 94,
  108, 142; customs,
  decay of, 65-67; perpateh,
  19; See also culture
administration, 145; See
  also government
administrative unit, village
  as, 38
adult education, 59
agriculture, 69; products,
  69; techniques, 61-62
Aidit, 34
alcohol, 46
Americans, 33
appliances, electric, 40, 43
Arabic (language) 141, 142;
  script, 54-55, 59, 64, 152;
  See also Arabs; Jawi script
Arabs, 5; culture, 35, 141;
  music, 35; physical appearance, 35; poetry, 35; See
  also Arabic (language)
arithmetic, 62-63; Western,
  62

army, 104, 107; Reserve, 35
attitudes, village concerning
  economic activities, 70-108

Bangi, 21, 24, 25, 39-41, 42,
  43, 59, 78-79, 113
bangsa, 23, 24, 35-36, 37, 52,
  79, 123, 135, 138-41
Banjarese, 23, 79, 132-33,
  135
bargaining, 26-27, 91
Barisan Socialis Party, 57
Batak, 8
behavior, v, vi; interpersonal,
  125-26, 142-44; ritual, 144
Bengal, 14
Berita Harian, 54
bersilat, 67
betel, 101, 105, 116, 118n., 157
bicycles, 40, 114
bilal, 134, 140, 141-42
boats, building, 95; poling,
  110
bomoh (medicine men), 43, 80
boundaries, cultural, 1; national, 1

-165-

Indians, vi, 2, 5, 8, 9, 10,
23, 65; economic roles of,
15-16; influence of, 13-
16; as laborers, 7-8, 14-
15, 68; relations with, 13-
16; settlement of, 14-16;
social role of, 15-16;
stereotypes of, 17, 30-31;
as storekeepers, 5, 40,114,
139
individual, importance of,
125, 136, 145-46
Indonesia, 5, 8-9, 34, 38-
39; and Indonesians, 4,
33; villagers' knowledge
of, 52-53
industrialization, 151
influences, 5, 13-16, 59-
64, 105-06, 142-43;
Buddhist, 13; cultural, 5;
of education, 59-64; Indian,
13-16; religions, 142-43; of
women, 105-06, 142
information, sources of, 17,
18, 32
Information Officer, 56
Information Services, 56
inheritance, 145
initiative, 68-69, 128-30;
of Chinese, 68-69; of
women, 128-30
interaction, of villagers with
outsiders, 35-37; See also
contact
intermarriage, 8-9; with
Javanese, 23; with Senoi,
31
interpersonal behavior, pattern of, 125-26; standards
of, 142-44

interpersonal relationships, v,
146-47
Ipoh, 46-47, 127
irrigation, 19, 22
Islam, vii, 5, 6, 25, 31, 46,
55, 64, 91, 94, 124, 136,
143, 144, 152; code of, 132,
142; ideals of, 97; villagers'
involvement with, 64-65;
values of, 142

Jakun, 2, 4
jalanjalan, 51, 105, 127; See
also visiting
Jambi, 14
Japanese, 38
Java, 8, 10
Javanese, 13-14, 21, 22-23;
trade, 5-6
Jawi (Arabic) script, 54-55, 59,
64, 152
Jelebu, 27, 98
Jendram Hilir, v, 17-23, 26,
27, 31, 32, 33, 34, 35-36,
38, 41, 42, 49, 78, 97, 99,
108, 113, 115, 124-25, 126,
127, 137, 138, 141, 145, 153,
152 and passim; education in,
59-64; and national organiza-
tions, 57-59; settlement of,
110-11
Jendram Ulu, 17-23, 36, 80,
102, 114, 124, 129, 141
jewelry, 90, 91, 92
Johore, 4, 6, 7, 9, 70
jungle products, 31

Kajang, 19, 21, 22, 26, 38,
39, 41-45, 56, 78, 82, 100,
111, 113, 137, 150, population

Prime Minister, 34, 111-12,
116; See also Mentri Besar
protection, British, 7
Public Works Department, 15,
40, 139

quarrying, 69
Queen, 116

racial groups, 32, 37
radio, 34-35, 50, 53-54,
57, 65, 104, 130, 138;
propaganda, 34-35, 53-54
Radio Djakarta, 34, 53-54
Radio Malaysia, 34, 53
Raffles, Stamford, 11
railways, 40
Raja, 18, 110, 133
Ramadan, 89, 142, 143
Ramba, 18, 110-11, 138-40
Rawa, 8
reactions, of villagers, 3-4;
to Chinese, 3-4; to Indians,
3; to other ethnic groups, 3
reciprocity, 147-48
relationships, of villagers, v,
vi, 95-98, 125, 132, 146-
47; with Chinese, 23-30, 41;
economic, 95-98, 106-07;
with Indonesians, 33; interpersonal, 95-98, 125, 132,
146-47; with outside world,
v, vi, 23-30, 31, 33, 37, 38,
41, 111-12, 147-48, 153; with
Senoi, 31; social, vii, 95-98,
106-07, 122-24, 127-28, 145-
53; with state, 111-12; with
storekeepers, 41
religion, vii, 38, 112, 145, 152;
organization of, in village, 38,
112, 145; See also ritual

religious festivals, expense of,
88-90
Resident, 7
rezeki, 106
rice, See padi
RIDA boatyard, 95, 107
rituals, 93, 127, 144; See also
ceremonial
river banks, 109-10
roads, 113
rubber, 15, 22, 68, 110; estates,
8, 18, 71; production, 24, 41,
56, 71-98, 150; smallholdings, 19, 62, 68, 71, 74-76;
tapping, v, 61, 70-71, 92-
93, 145; trees, 71, 150
Rumi (Roman) script, 54-55, 59
rural development, 39, 61-64
rural population, 1, 10, 13,
36, 69, 71, 109, 150-53;
living standards of, 71

Sabah, 32, 35
"Sakai," See Senoi
Sanskrit, 13, 14
Sarawak, 32, 35
saudara, 34, 51, 96, 107, 126
schools, 59-64, 115, 150; school
teachers, 103, 115, 134, 136-
38; See also education
scripts, 54-55, 59, 138; Jawi
(Arabic), 54-55, 59, 64, 152;
Rumi, 54-55, 59
sekolah kebangsaan (primary
school), 59, 60, 115
Selangor, 7, 8, 9, 11, 51, 70,
109, 145
Semang, 2, 4
Senoi ("Sakai"), 2, 4, 18, 31,
35

travel, 50-52, 56
trees, rubber, 71, 150
Trengganu, 7, 9, 14,
  34, 51, 70, 127
tribal groups, 32
trickery, 26-27
Tumasek, 5
Tunku Abdul Rahman,
  Prime Minister, 34

Ulu Langat, 41, 111
UMNO, See United Malay
  National Organization
United Malay National Or-
  ganization (UMNO), 57,
  111, 138
University of Malaya, 56
urban Malays, 45-50, 95,
  108, 136; life of, 38-50
Utusan Melayu, 54-55

values, village, v, vii, 3,
  70-108, 142-43, 152-53;
  economic, 70-108; hier-
  archy of, 127-28; Islamic,
  142; moral, 124; religious,
  142-43; sentimental, 124;
  social, 124, 149; sociological basis for, 108, 109-44
vegetable growing, 82, 99-101
Vietnam, 1
Vigilante Corps, 58-59
village agent, 79
villagers, v, vi, vii, 18, 70-
  108, 109; attitudes of, 70-
  108; daily lives of, 71-108,
  124-25, 142, 146-53; stereotypes of, 17-37
violence, 50

visiting, 47, 48, 50-52, 57,
  104-05, 127; See also
  jalanjalan
visual aids, 63

Wak, 133
warfare, 38
weeds (lalang), 62, 73-74, 82,
  99
west coast, 145
Western culture, 60-64, 111,
  148-49; and dress, 143-44;
  and values, 149
white people, 32-33
women, 50-52, 90-92, 104-
  06, 122-23, 128-30, 142-44,
  150; dress of, 143-44; influence of, 142, 150; status of,
  104-06, 122-23, 128-30, 143
Women's Institute, 57-58, 115
wood carving, 66
working habits, village, 77-78,
  103

Yang di-Pertuan Agong, 112
Yap Ah Loy, 13